Jon Smith

Digital Marketing for Businesses

includes social media marketing

In easy steps is an imprint of In Easy Steps Limited
16 Hamilton Terrace · Holly Walk · Leamington Spa
Warwickshire · United Kingdom · CV32 4LY
www.ineasysteps.com

Notice of Liability
Every effort has been made to ensure that this book contains accurate
and current information. However, In Easy Steps Limited and the
author shall not be liable for any loss or damage suffered by readers
as a result of any information contained herein.

Trademarks
All trademarks are acknowledged as belonging to their respective
companies.

In Easy Steps Limited supports The Forest Stewardship Council (FSC),
the leading international forest certification organization. All our titles
that are printed on Greenpeace approved FSC certified paper carry the
FSC logo.

MIX
Paper from
responsible sources
FSC® C020837

Printed and bound in the United Kingdom

ISBN 978-1-84078-863-1

Contents

10 Instagram 155

11 Facebook 175

1 Introduction to digital marketing

Digital marketing is a catch-all term for all of your online marketing activities. Gone are the days when building a website was enough – you need to let potential customers know you exist and ensure they come back again and again.

Why digital marketing?

Quite simply, it's no longer possible to consider marketing without considering digital. Consumers are always connected – be it on their desktops, laptops, tablets or mobile devices. In fact, consumers are even "second screening" – i.e. engaging with their phone whilst watching TV or working on their laptop – which means if your brand isn't part of the conversation or available across all devices immediately, it's likely your product or service won't even be considered and another more digitally aware company will enjoy growth at your expense.

If you're a business owner intent on finding new customers and retaining the ones you have, no matter what product or service you provide, you will need to have a digital marketing strategy. Granted – there will be aspects you will utilize more than others but an awareness of what's out there, and how it works, will make it much easier to decide which methods you should use to reach your potential customer base.

Don't forget

Digital marketing is an ever-changing discipline – keep abreast of new developments by visiting HubSpot's blog: **https:// blog.hubspot.com/**

Digital marketing moves fast – every month there are new tools, platforms and apps being launched to help business owners achieve their goals. So, how does a book about digital marketing avoid becoming outdated? Simple. This book shows you the disciplines and mindset you need to employ to market your business successfully – the apps and platforms mentioned will change and improve over time, but the techniques and the fundamentals will remain pertinent, valid and effective.

Can I master digital?

Of course! By both understanding and approaching each aspect of digital in a structured way, and by using this book as your guide, you will be able to apply the same techniques to your own particular business and reap the rewards.

This book looks at the underlying principles behind each of the key aspects of digital marketing, namely:

- **Content marketing**
- **Social marketing**
- **Search marketing**
- **Customer journey**

Then, of course, how to measure it all. It will help you to define what your goals are and provide a structured way for you to achieve them – whether that's acquiring new leads, converting leads into customers, retaining the customers you already have, and creating brand champions (or even communities of advocates) who like your business and/or products so much, they feel compelled to tell others.

Content marketing

Content marketing has become a core marketing activity for many businesses. For small businesses, sharing useful content online offers a powerful way to engage with customers – via blogs, case studies and email newsletters. At the same time, social media is helping businesses distribute their content – as videos, infographics and more are all shared via social media platforms like Twitter, LinkedIn, Pinterest, Instagram and Facebook.

Sharing relevant, interesting and valuable content allows your business to build relationships with your customers. By sharing useful information that solves your customers' problems, you can improve your customer service and inspire loyalty and trust.

By providing evidence that you can meet your promises – such as case studies and testimonials – you can also convince prospects to become customers without having to resort to a hard sell.

Today, everyone expects to find the answers to their questions on your website. The right content can demonstrate your expertise, show you understand your customers and their needs, and position you as a leader in your field.

Marketing content works incredibly hard for businesses. It can show your brand values and prove that you're up-to-date in your field. What's more, it can attract more website visitors, improve your search rankings, and widen your reach.

Beware

A good content marketing strategy won't be created overnight – you will need to invest in resources to have the very best content that drives business success.

Social marketing

Social media marketing has many platforms that you can use, and it can be difficult to decide which platforms are right for your business. With its ability to reach audiences, social media marketing is rapidly positioning itself at the core of many brands' marketing strategies. Despite the plethora of social platforms that seem to appear every few months, there are five main platforms that offer businesses a unique set of opportunities: Facebook, Instagram, Twitter, LinkedIn, and Pinterest.

Social media marketing **is** time consuming, especially if you want to do it well. Yes – you can automate posting to these networks with the various scheduling tools available, but to maximize your brand awareness and customer retention efforts it needs to be managed daily. Plus, only posting your own content will just irritate users; social media is also about reposting informative and entertaining content from your wider industry to your users.

Increasingly, companies are posting images and photographs of their teams at work, representing a "human" element to their business that is paramount to consumer buying decisions. Furthermore, to really reach consumers, social media advertising is an excellent way to reach consumers beyond those who do not follow your brand.

Don't be disheartened – the time you spend marketing your business via social is time well spent. Using the techniques and advice in this book, you can quickly position your business as a leader in your space, engage with customers, and gain valuable feedback about your products and service by being part of the conversation.

There are specific chapters in this book looking in depth at each of the social media channels.

Check out Chapter 4 – SEM & SEO to get the most out of search.

Search marketing

Search marketing (sometimes referred to as search engine marketing or SEM) encompasses search engine optimization (SEO) and paid advertising. And, frustratingly, it is these abbreviations and the jargon that surrounds the industry (CPC – cost per click, CPA – cost per acquisition, CPL – cost per lead, and CPM – cost per thousand) that tend to alienate business owners from dipping their feet in the water when it comes to embarking on a search marketing campaign.

But if you can understand the terminology, you can understand how you too will be able to make search marketing an integral and important part of your digital marketing mix. We will explore search marketing in greater depth later in the book.

In summary, SEO is the practice of earning traffic through unpaid or free listings, while paid advertising is buying traffic through paid search listings.

Paid search ads help marketers get more web traffic via desktop or mobile web search. It's instant, it's effective, and you have complete control of your budget.

SEO is the generic term for a number of techniques you can use to help search engines better understand your web pages and ensure that when a user is searching for something relating to you or your business, it's your web page that appears high up on page 1 of the search results pages (SERPs).

Measuring digital

As with any aspect of business, it's important to measure what you are doing to know if it's having a positive impact. With digital marketing everything is trackable, traceable and measurable, which means that you will know very quickly which aspects of your digital marketing campaigns are working and which are not.

It is this level of visibility that makes digital marketing such an exciting aspect of running a business, and why – even if you feel you're new to many of the topics contained within this book – you should take the plunge and give it a go.

There's an old marketing adage that goes: "Half the money I spend on advertising is wasted; the trouble is I don't know which half." This can be true with traditional magazine, radio and billboard advertising but it's not the case with digital – whether you measure success as Facebook "likes", or new leads for your sales team to contact, or actual sales via your website, what you spend on digital marketing can be closely attributed to specific campaigns and channels, meaning that you're no longer operating blind.

In Chapter 15 we'll take a closer look at Google Analytics – a critical tool that will help you manage and monitor your digital marketing success. We'll also look at the essential metrics you will need to become familiar with to monitor your social media presence.

The importance of social

Social media has exploded in recent years. We have now entered the age of the relationship. With the help of social media, marketing has evolved into a two-way dialogue, not just a monologue. By using social media as a way to advertise your product or service offering, you can speak directly to the consumers in an arena they are comfortable with. Social media allows businesses to connect with their customers and prospects while shaping their perceptions of products and services.

Social media can be extremely powerful for business. But it can also be a big risk as well. Social media is not a fix-all, and if your service is weak, your products are poor, and you do not respond quickly enough to those business failures, then your customers will use social media to enhance and vocalize those feelings for the world to see. Not being online does not take the problem away. Customers will still air their issues online; you just need to make sure that you are also online, and implementing a listening strategy so you can nip any grievances in the bud quickly and efficiently before the problem escalates.

Beware

People will talk about you and your business, whether you are on social media platforms or not.

Hot tip

Set up a listening strategy for your company name.

So, before you begin with your social marketing strategy and begin to explore the wider world of content marketing, it's crucial that you set up an effective listening strategy for your business.

Your listening strategy

Google Alerts is a service that allows you to receive email alerts on any keyword or phrase you wish to monitor. Whilst it doesn't catch everything, it's a free service, and you can turn up some gems so it's well worth the time it takes to set it up. You can elect to receive alerts as often as you like. The more specific your search phrase, the more relevant the results. However, Google Alerts is not the same as it used to be, and it is likely that it will eventually be another tool that Google will terminate, in a similar way that they switched off so many excellent Google products such as Google Reader, etc. In addition, Google Alerts only sends you emails if new articles, web pages or blog posts make it into the top 10 Google news results, the top 20 Google web search results, or the top 10 Google blog search results for your query. If the top results remain the same for a while, you will not receive emails on your topic. For this reason, there's a great product called "Mention", which will monitor and listen to what is being said about you or your company online.

How to get started with Mention

Go to the homepage (**www.mention.com**) and click the **Start your free trial** button to get started with your 14-day free trial. You can sign up using your existing Facebook, Twitter, Google, or LinkedIn account, or just enter your name, email address, and a password to create a new account.

Google Alerts is good to get started, but you'll need a more robust listening tool such as Mention to truly have your ear to the ground

Register with **mention.com** to perfect your listening strategy.

If you sign up using an existing account, you'll be asked to enter an email address. Then, you can choose which brands you'd like to receive alerts for. The Mentions are displayed according to the keywords or phrases that you've chosen for your alert.

...cont'd

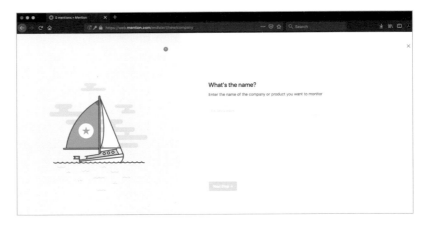

Creating a new alert on Mention

Once you've set up your account, you'll be prompted to create alerts for your own brand/product and those of your competitors. You should set up alerts for your own company and products, as well as for those of your main competitors and for the main players within your chosen industry.

Your own brand/name: Get started with Mentions of your own brand or name to get immediate feedback on where your company name is being mentioned on the web.

Choose your languages: English is the default, but you can choose to receive alerts in French, Spanish, German and many other languages too. You can also manage and filter your sources. You could receive alerts from all sources (the web, Facebook, Twitter, news, blogs, videos, forums and images) but you can exclude some of those sources if you wish, or block a specific site.

Set up alerts for your competitors' names and industry news.

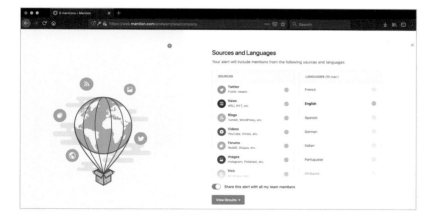

Expand your listening reach: If you do decide to pay for Mention, I suggest creating additional Mention alerts for key staff members' names along with key figures that operate within your industry. You can also set up alerts for industry news, more competitors, and individual product names, etc.

...cont'd

Choose your influencers: You can now create your own lists of influencers. This will allow you to organize and keep an eye on your existing brand ambassadors and the influencers you want to work with in the future.

Hot tip

By monitoring influencers in your industry, you'll have an endless supply of content ideas.

Include and exclude expressions: Type in the words or phrases that you want to get alerts for. You can include common misspellings or variations, and you can also exclude terms – i.e. tell Mention not to send you alerts for pages that include a given word or phrase. For example, I have a particularly common name and there are a number of people tweeting under the name "Jon Smith" so I have excluded all of the other Jon Smith Twitter accounts from my summary email.

Mention notifications

Mention also sends you an email when you have new results:

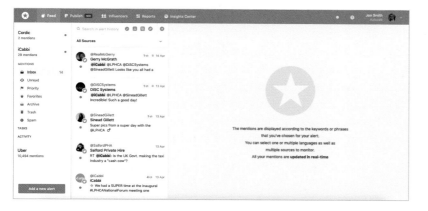

Beware

After your 14-day trial has ended, you will be charged to use Mention.

As you can see, the Mention application is much more user friendly and it also has more options than Google Alerts. Click on any of the links to read the Mention, mark it as a favorite or delete the Mention.

In the far left column, you have a list of views. The default view is Mentions, which you can see in the next column, with the most recent Mention at the top.

You can filter the Mentions column by source, and toggle the view between All, Unread, and Priority.

On the right, in the main view, you get a preview of the page with your Mention. This is really cool because you can see the context of the Mention without having to actually visit the page – it's obviously much more robust than the little search-style snippet you get in the Google Alerts email. From this view you can choose to click through to the original URL or the source, and you can also "favorite" the Mention, block the source, or trash it using the little icons at the top.

Is there a cost to Mention?

Yes. Mention is a paid-for service. At the time of going to press, Mention offers a 14-day free trial with prices then starting at $25 per month for a single user, with more comprehensive starter and enterprise packages available. Visit **https://mention.com/en/pricing/** to find the latest prices.

Your social media success

It is interesting to see what people consider to be the steps to social media success. Some people just see the numbers. For example, they look at a Twitter account that has 20,000 followers, or they view a Facebook page that has thousands of "likes", and they assume that they are successful in their social media activities. This is not quite true! Social media is successful if you are communicating and building relationships with your target market, which will ultimately convert into new business. There is no point in a kitchen designer from Northamptonshire, UK or Des Moines, Iowa having 3,000 likes on their Facebook page if those likes are all from people in Cambodia.

Social media success will rarely happen overnight. When you break it down, there are really only four steps to achieve social media success online:

1 **Build & maintain your platforms**

The oft-used phrase, "If you build it, they will come" is a cliché, but there is no getting away from the fact that if your platforms are not professionally designed, if you have an inactive or poorly designed website, or have not bothered to change your Twitter profile picture from the generic "egg" picture, then this will have an effect on your overall strategy.

2 **Grow your network**

It is a well-known fact that if you do not have a network of people to talk to online, then you are really just talking to yourself! Have a strategy for growing your network online for each platform. Decide and define who your target market is and start to follow them. Use tools such as **www.followerwonk.com** to find people on Twitter. Run some adverts on Facebook to see how to grow your audience. Make sure that your strategy is ongoing and reviewed at least every six weeks. These tools will be covered in more detail later in the book, as well as giving you more inspirational ideas on how to build your following, connections and "likes".

Social media is not a numbers game.

Review your platforms at least once every six weeks.

3 **Define a listening, engagement and content strategy**

This is probably the area of digital marketing where most businesses fail. Their posts are all over the place, with no consistency. They fail to set up listening strategies to respond to people who are talking about them online (good and bad). Try **mention.com** (see pages 17-21), which offers a 14-day free trial, to help you listen to your audience. The scattergun approach to producing content does not work.

Make sure that you are using a social media management system such as Hootsuite (**www.hootsuite.com** – a social media scheduling platform that allows you to prepare your social posts in advance and have them post automatically when you want) or TweetDeck (**www.tweetdeck.com** – a tool to help you manage and monitor multiple Twitter timelines in one interface), and start planning what you are going to say and do. Decide on a blogging topic for the month and plan what you are going to write about, with set dates for publication.

But the most important strategy in Step 3 is the word "engagement". Thank people for mentioning you in a tweet, ask people questions, comment on others' posts, etc. You must talk to people in order to build those important relationships that lead to business and referrals.

4 **Measure the results**

As with any type of marketing, whether it is printing leaflets, your website activity, or special offers, etc., as we've learned earlier in this chapter, you need to measure the results, and social media activity is no different. If you don't know what is working and what is not working then how do you know if it is successful? Whilst vanity metrics such as number of "likes" and followers have a place, you need to be going to the next level and measuring engagement – what is the number of people exposed to your social media content who are going on to be customers of your business?

Hot tip

Plan your content topics in advance. Write the topics down for each month and then gear your content posts around those topics.

23

Don't forget

Don't forget the word "social". It is important to engage and talk to others online for a successful social media strategy.

...cont'd

Remember Einstein's famous quote:

> " *Insanity: doing the same thing over and over again and expecting different results.* "
>
> albert einstein

It makes good business sense to make sure that you are measuring your activities. As we've seen, if it's digital then it's trackable, traceable, and accountable, meaning that the data is there to accurately measure and draw conclusions – throughout this book we'll show you how to find and interpret this data to help you make sound business decisions, each and every time.

Check your Google Analytics account (see Chapter 15) to see how much traffic is being generated by your social media activities. You may be pleasantly surprised. Simply click **Acquisition**, then **Social** to view the results.

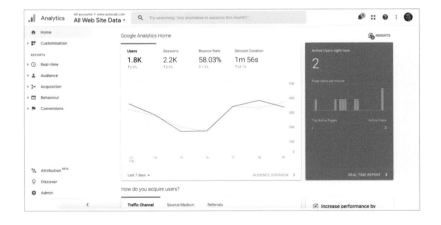

Setting your digital marketing goals

So many companies are "winging it" when it comes to social activity. The expression "social media ROI" has many names – for example, "return on investment" and "return on influence", to name but a few – but do you really know what you are trying to achieve by having an effective social media strategy?

Where do you start and how do you relate what to measure online with your overall business goals?

We will discuss 10 reasons that businesses, small and large, are active online. Read through each goal and then choose just two of those goals before you indulge in the rest of this book. Once you decide where you are going, you will have a better vision of how you are going to get there.

Most people will answer the question "Why are you doing social media?" with "To get more sales". Many of the reasons below will result in more sales. Therefore, this has been removed as a reason to be active online.

To drive traffic to your website

If the majority of your sales come from your website, then it is a no-brainer to have this goal as top of your list. Traffic to your website is important for all businesses, but especially important if you are selling your products or services online.

You can create an amazing website that looks stunning and is extremely functional. However, without traffic to the site you are going nowhere fast.

Using social media to drive traffic to your website is easy:

- **Twitter**. You can embed the link to your website in a tweet.

> ISV Software Ltd @ISVSoftwareLtd · Jul 30
> 80% of women feel their employer is supportive of them but 44% say their gender has hindered their career - ow.ly/zzBeH

(Check out Chapter 12 for help with Twitter.)

Setting your digital marketing goals and objectives is the first stage to social media success.

Use a URL shortener (see pages 217-218) to gain statistics on how often a link has been clicked on from your social networking sites.

...cont'd

- **Facebook**. In Chapter 11, we will talk through how to post a link to your website on Facebook, which is also a highly effective way to drive traffic back to your website. You can also use the Facebook applications or Facebook adverts to achieve similar results.

 Connections Employment Agency Limited shared a link.
3 hours ago

New Job
Warehouse Operative / Counterbalance FLT Driver - Trafford Park, Trafford Park, England, £16000 per annum

 **Warehouse Operative / Counterbalance FLT Driver - Trafford Park**
Warehouse Operative/Counterbalance FLT Driver job in Trafford Park Counterbalance FLT Licence - Essential Reach

- **LinkedIn**. Post updates into your LinkedIn status update to drive traffic back to your blog, products online, or any part of your website. We'll cover this in Chapter 13.

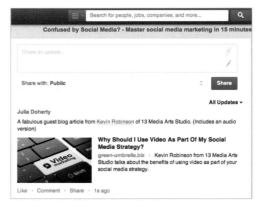

There are many ways in which you can use social media to drive traffic back to your website. Always check that your website is visible in the "About us" areas of your online profiles or biographies for additional opportunities.

To appear an expert in your field

Everybody trusts an expert! As every salesperson will tell you, individuals want to do business with people they know, like, and trust.

The best way to brand yourself as an expert is by using a strategy that leverages social media. This includes LinkedIn, Twitter, Facebook, YouTube, and top of the pile is blogging. We will go into more detail in Chapter 3 on how you can appear an expert in your field within each platform.

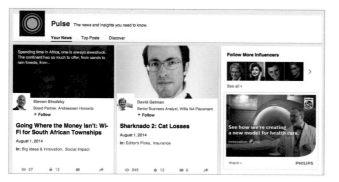

Did you know that you can publish articles on LinkedIn and become an influencer? What a fabulous way to appear a subject matter expert! If you have a longer piece of writing, instead of writing a post, write an article (see page 234 for more information about this).

Brand awareness

There are many reasons that brand awareness may be top of your social media goals. You may be a fledgling company that is dipping its toes in the business world, or you may have been established for many years with a solid customer base and are now looking to expand into different markets. Perhaps you have a new product to launch, or a new service to sell to a niche market.

Reputation management

Social media helps a brand reach out to their customers and communicate with them, playing a significant role in online reputation management. 70% of people who look for reviews online trust posts by friends and family, while 90% trust reviews from other consumers. From a business-to-business (B2B) point of view, 42% of people look up the people that they are going to do business with, and 45% of people learnt something from searching online, which changed their minds. (*Source:* **https:// statuslabs.com/reputation-management-stats-2020**) What better place to be constantly looking for reviews than social media?

Don't forget to give away your knowledge and expertise as much as possible to gain credibility.

Provide videos on YouTube to show your expertise in a particular subject, sector or industry. See pages 36-37 for more on creating effective videos.

Make sure all your platforms are branded professionally.

...cont'd

Surveys (**http://ow.ly/tt6Mw**) tell us that 22% of people who have had a bad experience are likely to comment about it online, while only 9% of people who have had a good experience will do the same. All these numbers point to a growing trend where the reputation of a business online directly impacts bottom-line revenue.

Having a strategy for reputation management is key for many businesses, especially in the service industry. Perhaps you have bought a business from a previous owner who did not have a brilliant reputation, in which case having "reputation management" as your main social media goal should be top of your list.

To keep an eye on the competition

If it is important to find out what kind of customers your competitors are targeting, or what their social media marketing strategy looks like, then the reason "keeping an eye on your competitors" should be toward the top of your list.

As important as it is to keep an eye on the competition, many small business owners don't know much about what their competitors are doing to reach customers. The benefits of watching your competitors are almost immediate – you learn what you can do to make your business unique, you see their weaknesses (i.e. customer service issues), and you get great ideas to improve your own strategy.

You can set up Twitter lists for all of your competitors (see the Twitter lists section in Chapter 12 on how to set up lists).

It is easy to keep an eye on the competition on Facebook by clicking the **Follow** button on their page and choosing from the options in the drop-down menu, so you do not miss any posts. Once you have done this, for any posts that appear on their page, you will see a red notification symbol on your personal profile.

Don't forget you do not need to actually follow your competitors on Twitter – you simply add them to a list.

To uncover new opportunities and meet new people

Expanding your customer base has always been expensive, and it may be even more so today. In an uncertain economic climate, few companies seem ready to take the risk of starting out with new suppliers. Instead, it makes sense to look for new opportunities in industries where you are already doing business.

If new sales are top of your list, then this should be your number-one goal. Your social media strategy for uncovering new opportunities will be based on listening and engagement.

There are many strategies to gain opportunities for potential new sales. These are covered in the detailed chapters for each platform later in the book.

Customer loyalty

If you are struggling to retain customers and find yourself having to search for new clients, then customer loyalty will be important to you. Implement a social media strategy to ensure customer retention and loyalty.

There are many ways to keep in contact with your customers online.

- Make sure that you are tagging your customers in posts that are relevant to them. Here is an example of how you can do this on Facebook:

Tag the business in the post

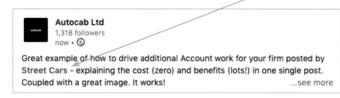

- Feed your customers with regular free content utilizing your blog and social networking platforms.
- Set up Twitter lists for your current clients.
- You can tag your clients in all platforms to say that it was good to meet with them, retweet their messages to your network, or share their blog articles on your LinkedIn page, etc.

Remember to use the tagging facility on all networks to ensure that your customer will see the post.

...cont'd

- Have a listening strategy set up for potential customer complaints so that you can react quickly. Providing a first-class service online will always help with customer retention.

To get news instantaneously

If you are a local business, then having a listening strategy for local news is key. You may be in an industry that constantly needs to be ahead of the game to be successful. Therefore, this is the goal for you.

- Are you following your local newspapers and radio stations online?
- Do you have notifications set up for your local town?

To help improve your search results

Search remains the main way in which many people discover a business, and search engine optimization (SEO) (find out more in Chapter 4) should be a key part of your online communications strategy. An active presence on social media, and sharing and distributing keyword-rich content, will improve your placing on Google and other search engines, ensuring that more people find you online.

Social media is the future of communications

Social media is not a fad and it is not going away. Millennials – your next pool of employees, customers, and competitors – prefer to use text messaging and the social web over any other form of communication. It is the natural evolution of communications. If you are not involved in social media at this stage, then you will simply be playing catch-up in a few years' time or your business will not exist.

The social web is where a generation is going to connect, learn and discover. Ignore this at your peril! You have got to be in it to win it! Here are some examples of what we do at **In Easy Steps**:

Facebook

Twitter

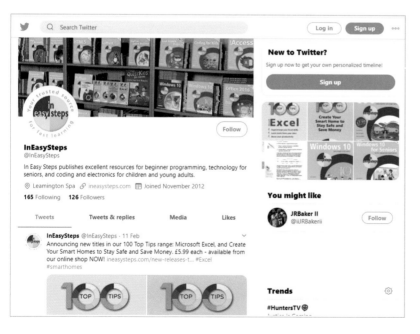

...cont'd

Website

Pinterest

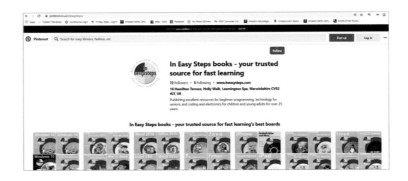

LinkedIn

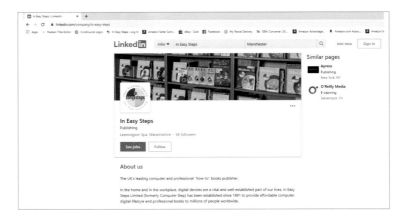

2 Content is king

The sure-fire way to win over customers to your brand, product and service is through well-written, attractive and value-added content. Find out how you can use content to generate sales and retain customers.

Content = customers

With the sheer number of companies out there providing a similar or the same product or service that you do, it's essential that customers are able to find you and understand just how you are different. That comes from creating new and original content to engage with your audience.

Keep it fresh!

Part of any content strategy should include resources for revisions and updates. Content can quickly become tired, stale or even incorrect as legislation changes, new products are released by your competitors, and other changes happen in your wider industry. Be sure to review your content regularly and know that sometimes it's better to retire older content completely than dilute the great new stuff you are producing with out-of-date material that might hurt your brand more than help, in the eyes of your prospects.

Content calendar

Struggling to think of what content to create? Start with major cultural festivals and holidays, awareness days, trade shows and awards nights in your industry – making your brand, product or service relevant to the lives of your audience.

Use third party experts

Try creating a range of content to find out what works best for your audience. You may be a skilled writer but not too good with video – don't worry; there are legions of agencies and freelancers able to help you create and execute the perfect content strategy.

Hot tip

Stay abreast of what's trending on social – and tie your brand in to the latest fad to get people talking about you.

Your content arsenal

To sell successfully online you'll need not only a comprehensive understanding of the customer journey in order to create the right lead-generating content, but also an understanding of what types of content assets – i.e. case studies, testimonial videos, blogs, articles, infographics, and ebooks – you should be creating to attract, engage, and ultimately convert visitors into paying customers.

Good content marketing obviously relies on you producing great content that is attractive, easy-to-digest, and adds value to the reader, but critically, it also relies on having a great strategy in terms of which pieces of content to use at which stage of the customer journey.

Let's take a closer look at some of the types of content you should start using to attract the highest possible number of visitors to your website.

Hot tip

Write the longer-form article first, then look at using extracts or snippets to create Twitter posts, Facebook updates, and shorter articles.

Blogs

Blogs are covered in some detail in Chapter 3. Therefore, in summary, blogs are short, written pieces of content (aim for between 800-2,000 words) that should focus on presenting and answering a single pain point that your prospects need resolving. Blogs work best for prospects both at the awareness and the consideration stage of the buyer journey. A good blog post will outline a challenge or pain point your prospect may or may not know that they face, and then show them clearly how it can be resolved. Aim to write a new blog post about once a week.

As shy as you and the team might be, a "behind the scenes at the office" video will always gain a lot of views.

Video content

Pictures say a thousand words and videos say much, much more... If content is king, then video is the king of content.

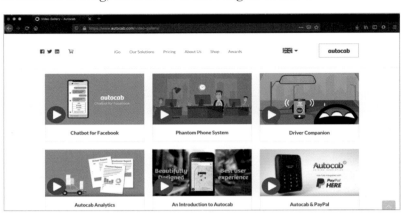

Why video works

Your prospects are all busy people fighting through a glut of online content to find the answers to their questions, and video provides information in an easy-to-digest format perfectly suited for mobile and desktop consumption. Whether it's a two-minute animated explainer video, a behind-the-scenes day at your office, a product review, or a how-to video, prospects will often check out your video content before they'll commit to downloading and reading your beautifully crafted ebook or white paper. So, make sure you place your videos front and center. Let your imagination run wild and don't be afraid to inject a bit of humor.

Video content works across all three stages of the customer journey – from first introduction of your product or service through to how-to videos to help with onboarding, or technical support videos for retention.

Get professional help

Whether it's filming in your office, or creating a two-minute animated "explainer" video, a quick search online will reveal a whole host of professional videographers and animators who can help you with your video content. Just like with the images on your website, if your video content is sub-par it will affect your online reputation and give potential customers cause to pause before purchasing from you.

Use video throughout your site

Although it's a great idea to have a specific video library containing all of your video content, don't assume your users will find it. In addition, allow users to access your video content where it will have the most impact. In the example below, the Chatbot video is shown at the top of the Chatbot product page, allowing users to get a short video introduction to the product before committing to reading more:

Depending on how you want to configure your website, users can watch the video within the same page, or clicking on the video takes users to the video on YouTube:

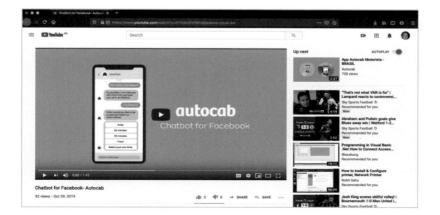

Images

They say that a picture says a thousand words (whoever "they" are), and they'd be right! Images, and good images at that, are absolutely essential on a website. They help break up a page of text. They confirm that you are writing about the same thing that the user thinks they are reading about. And they can explain things in far less time than it will take you to write about them and the reader has to read.

Use low-resolution images on a web page rather than high-resolution ones.

38

Protect your images

If you want to use an image on your site, you must ensure that you have copyright permission to do so. Likewise, it is essential to protect your own images from copyright infringement. There are a number of techniques you can employ – using watermarks, which allow users to view your image, but show it belongs to you; only letting people download low-resolution versions of the image; and asking your web developers to turn off "Save picture as". If you have saved the image at 72 dpi (see next page), there is nothing really to worry about in terms of printing a copy of the image, because the quality on the printed page will usually be grainy.

Image is everything

Not only is the visual impact of your images important, it is essential that you ensure that the images are maximized for use on the internet. For once, the best is not necessarily the highest quality. Images on a computer monitor can look completely different from the same image printed out on paper. The quality of an image (assuming that it is a good photo or design in the first place) is determined by the pixel size and the number of pixels to be shown per inch (dots per inch, or dpi). When preparing images for printed material, the rule of thumb is to save the image with at least 300 (if not more) dots per inch. When you are altering images to be shown on a website, you must turn the dpi down. There is simply no point saving an image at more than 72 dpi because computer monitors cannot appreciate the difference. Those companies that insist on posting images on their site with a dpi of more than 72 are just slowing down the load speed of their images, and therefore the site. This will annoy users.

Hot tip

Use product or people names within the filename of every image to improve SEO ranking.

A trick first cornered by large e-commerce stores was to save a small, medium, and sometimes even a large image of every product on the server. This means that if a customer is just browsing, they can see a thumbnail image of everything in that category or section of the site. If the customer wants to read more about the product, they click on the link and it will bring them through to the product description page. On this page will be a slightly larger image, allowing the customer to scrutinize the product with more ease. Lastly, if the customer wants more, they can click on the image and it will bring them to another page showing the image at full-page size. This tactic helps keep your website working quickly, by providing the vast number of consumers with thumbnail images only, but also allows customers to see more of what they want, when they want.

Ebooks

A personal favorite of mine, ebooks are a great way to show your prospects your expertise in the subject matter, and also your ability to tell a story and take prospects on a journey.

Content within the ebook doesn't have to be as serious as a white paper, and nor does it have to be dense text over 100 pages in length. The best ebooks are quite short – maybe 10-15 pages – and contain a mixture of text and imagery that address a prospect's pain point and offer real solutions to buyers at the awareness stage of the buyer journey. Plan out your ebooks in advance (even if it's just proposed title/topic at this stage) and try to see if there are any thematic patterns between the ebooks you are planning. If so, you can create ebooks as part of a series, which you can incorporate within the cover and title. By producing a series of ebooks, it allows you to go back to prospects who've downloaded one in the past to alert them to the latest title, and quickly positions your business as the subject matter expert in your field.

In the example above, Autocab (**https://www.autocab.com/resources/**), a software provider to the taxi industry, offers free advice to taxi operators to help them utilize social media to generate awareness and passenger bookings. The ebook is popular because it gives business owners specific advice tailored to their industry – rather than generic tips and tricks – that can be executed immediately. The company promotes the ebook on social media channels such as Facebook and LinkedIn, as well as through search marketing and retargeting (see page 86), to generate interest in the company.

Don't forget

Ebooks should contain a mixture of text and visuals – use a designer to create the final look for maximum impact.

Hot tip

Mock up your ebook like a physical book – so much more appealing than a screenshot of a PDF document.

...cont'd

Unlike blogs, it's a good idea to "gate" your ebook content behind a landing page form. As you can see in this example, there are a number of ebooks available:

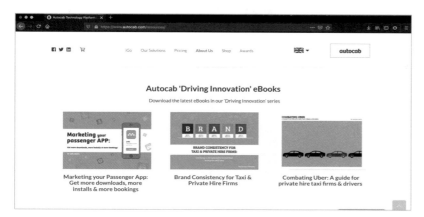

Ebooks must be maintained – schedule time in the year to double-check your content is still valid and correct.

To download an ebook, prospects must complete a form, provide their email address, and agree to receive marketing material from you (a General Data Protection Regulation (GDPR) requirement), and in return they gain access to your ebook.

If you are marketing to consumers based in Europe you must adhere to the General Data Protection Regulation (GDPR). Search "GDPR" on the internet to understand what you can and can't do with customer data.

This gives the customer access to the content, which hopefully they will find useful for their day-to-day business, but it also gives Autocab their contact details to be able to follow up with future ebook publication notifications and to begin to build a relationship that will, hopefully, result in a software sale when the customer continues along the customer journey.

A "pitch deck" is a set of presentation slides used to raise finance or sell to customers. Infographics work particularly well to explain complex ideas or present lots of numerical information in a simple-to-understand format.

Beware

Take your time creating infographics. If possible, find at least two sources for your numbers and make sure they're accurate.

Infographics

As marketers and business owners, we're usually data-driven and comfortable with numbers. But that doesn't mean your prospects are.

Bamboozling your readers with statistics makes written content a dense and often boring read. That's where infographics can play a big role in simplifying and condensing information in a visually engaging way. Infographics work well on a website, a pitch deck (see Hot tip), and on social media to make detailed information accessible to a wider audience. They can help raise awareness of your business or products and services, and successfully demonstrate your expertise and wider industry knowledge. The use of clever typography, graphs and charts to show statistics helps make valid points in a fraction of the time it takes for prospects to read through pages of text.

A search for "infographic template free" will return a treasure chest of editable templates you can use to create your own powerful set of infographics.

When deciding upon a style for your infographics, look for what helps explain the point you are trying to make, above and beyond what might be "cool" or trendy. Design styles are in a constant state of flux – 3D is cool and then it's not, flat design is all the rage and then it's not. If your infographic clearly displays the data and makes it easy for readers to understand, then it will have a shelf life way beyond what's hot right now.

Google struggles to understand the content embedded within an image – make sure there is text on the page explaining the highlights of the infographic so the page can be indexed (see page 137).

Brand your infographic so if it's shared, your company gets the credit for creating it.

As well as displaying numbers or statistics, infographics work well (as in the above example) to walk readers through a process or journey. Complex decision trees can be represented visually and allow readers to easily understand the salient points. If you run an e-commerce store, look at creating a graphic to explain your returns procedure – capture what your customer needs to do, but also give an indication of how long each stage takes.

Webinars

One of the most underutilized weapons in the marketer's arsenal is the webinar. A webinar is the perfect medium to talk through a number of prospect pain points either to a live audience who log on at the appointed time or, if you prefer, prerecorded, edited and released via your website.

Hot tip

Keep your webinars to under one hour, including Q&A.

A live webinar is interactive, with your attendees able to ask questions (via text chat) in real time that can be addressed by the webinar host there and then or during a Q&A session at the end. Webinars work best for those at the awareness and consideration stage, but have also been effective for those at the decision stage who are really looking for the final confirmation that your product or service addresses all their pain points and your company is the best provider on the market.

Webinars require pre-registration through a form that adds to your database of leads, and most webinar technology includes an analytics tool that will tell you who joined and for how long, making them a great lead generation and qualification tool.

Building up a bank of previous webinars that tackle a single subject is a great way to show you're an industry expert and the first point of call for potential customers looking for information. As with infographics, it's difficult for Google to index audio content, and therefore it's essential that you add text to the page that lists the topics covered in the webinar, and once the webinar has been broadcast, the key takeaways.

Case studies

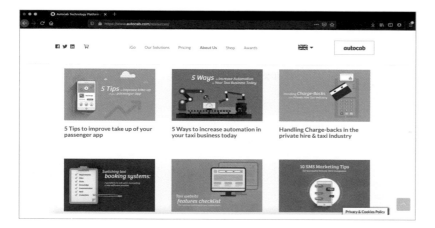

Don't forget to ask the case study subject for permission to use their company name, logo and information in your case study.

Case studies act as the proof of the pudding for most buyers. Prospects are wise to marketing techniques and aren't always wowed by your glitzy website and beautifully crafted content. They know you're talking about yourself, so embark on the buying journey with a healthy dose of skepticism. What most of us want to see, whether we're thinking of purchasing a paperback novel or a new customer relationship management (CRM) system, is what other "real people" thought of the product and service.

The same way customer reviews work so well in a business-to-consumer (B2C) environment, case studies provide the same power of persuasion in a business-to-business (B2B) environment. That other executives are willing to provide video or written testimony to your company's product or service, and your ability to deliver, speaks volumes in the eyes of prospects at the consideration stage. You can never have too many case studies, and whilst it takes some organizational effort to wrangle the interviews and prepare the content, the value for your business is priceless.

There is a temptation to write lots of short case studies (200-500 words) covering an array of topics in the hope that it improves SEO. However, go for quality over quantity as it's always the more comprehensive longer-form case study that ranks on the first page of Google, and that adds the most value to your prospects – which means a greater chance of them becoming paying customers.

Pricing tables

In Chapter 5 – The customer journey, we will learn that selling has changed. Gone are the days of the persuasive salesperson who held all the cards. Now, unless you're providing a consultancy or bespoke product, prospects expect to be able to access your pricing and specification documents easily via your website.

There is a school of thought that argues it's best to keep pricing hidden until the prospect has been wowed by their buyer journey and to only reveal pricing at the decision stage, so that they're less likely to walk away… but this shows a lack of respect for your prospect and insecurity in the value you place on your product or service. Far better to be upfront with your pricing from the outset. Those in the awareness and consideration stages need to know pricing to be able to move to the decision stage, so to not be upfront about it hampers rather than helps sales.

If your product really is beyond the budget of your prospect you've saved everyone a lot of wasted time and effort – it's costing you money to have a huge pipeline of leads and prospects who are ultimately going to baulk at your pricing later in the journey. Far better to have fewer prospects from the outset who have a greater chance of becoming opportunities.

In the example above, HubSpot offers three price points based on business size and, therefore, how many staff will need to access the software and the number of customers your business has. You can offer a single price point or choose to offer a range of pricing based on the features available, the number of user licenses you will provide, or a combination of both.

3 Blogging

Blogging provides an easy way to keep your brand top-of-mind with both potential and existing customers. Learn how to blog effectively and make blogging an essential part of your digital marketing offering.

What is a blog?

A blog is short for "web-log". A blog was originally created for people who like to produce journals, and therefore those who traveled and wanted to record their adventures would be seen as a blogger. Things have moved on since those early days, and a blog is so much more, nowadays. Here is the official definition of a blog:

blog
/bläg/ ◂))

noun

1. a personal website or web page on which an individual records opinions, links to other sites, etc. on a regular basis.

verb

1. add new material to or regularly update a blog.
"it's about a week since I last blogged"

What are the main differences between a blog and a regular website?

- Blogs are usually updated frequently, sometimes multiple times a day.
- When a web page is changed, that information is gone forever. However, with a blog the information stays online in chronological order.
- Blogs are easy to maintain. However, a website blogger may need an understanding of coding and other web skills.
- Blogs are used for communication, and they encourage people to join in discussions on a topic.
- There are whole communities of bloggers for specific industries, and this world is vibrant.
- Blogging gives you an instant way to publish your thoughts, opinions and ideas online.

The term "blog" was not coined until the late 1990s, which is when the internet really started to take off. When you analyze all of the points on the following pages and then look at the key factors that Google uses for search engine ranking (mainly refreshed content), you can see why blogging from a business perspective has been a positive step in the right direction.

Why is blogging important?

Blogging is important for all businesses. Whether you are a micro, small, or multinational organization, blogging should be integral to your online content marketing strategy. Here are the four main reasons that you should be blogging for your business:

Drive traffic to your website

Your blog gives you a platform to create relevant content for your clients and prospects. If used as a marketing tactic to drive traffic to your website it can be extremely powerful.

If driving traffic back to your website is a key strategy for your business, then make sure that your blog is either built into your website or is embedded in your website. If the blog is elsewhere online, then you may be providing valuable information that will attract traffic to your blog, not your website. Therefore, those visitors will not have the opportunity to explore your website or be attracted by one of your calls to action (CTAs) (see pages 62 and 133).

If your business is active on social networking sites such as Facebook, Twitter, Pinterest, LinkedIn or Instagram, then posting your article title (with an image) and a link, so that potential readers can click to read the full article and drive more traffic back to your site, is strongly recommended.

Here is a typical blog post on Facebook that will drive traffic back to Michael Hyatt's website:

Link to Michael's blog article

...cont'd

Hot tip

You can also use an excerpt when posting your blog. An excerpt is a "read more" link. So viewers receive a teaser in their email, but need to click to view the full article on your website.

Sorry Could You Say That Again? - The Benefit Of Video As A Social Tool

The chances are that if you are interested in this blog you probably, business, or you work for a company that want's you to reach out t When you come right down to it - that is the lifeblood of all busine out to people and basically we go..

Continue Reading...

Beware

Try not to manipulate the system by adding keywords where they are not appropriate. Your key focus should be on the user experience, not on how Google works.

Another way to attract traffic to your website using your blog is to utilize email. As mentioned in Chapter 1, it is important to capture those all-important email addresses from your website. Once captured, they can be stored on any type of email marketing software such as Mailchimp, Constant Contact, Infusionsoft, or something similar. If you're based in Europe, ensure you are GDPR compliant by requesting subscribers agree to receiving marketing messages from you when they give you their email address.

Increase your search engine optimization (SEO)

As mentioned in the previous section, having regular fresh content that is unique and not regurgitated is now the biggest influence for Google ranking. The easiest way to make sure you have new content on your website is to add a blog and then make regular contributions.

Use keywords in your articles. List the keywords, topics and categories you want your business to be found with. Use these words and related expressions when writing your posts.

Of course, whether you actively seek these out or not, blogging regularly about your business, industry, product or customer lifestyle will naturally increase your search keywords.

Keywords and topics on your website are a significant way in which Google (and other search engines) finds your site for these searched words.

Position your brand as an industry leader

Quality written articles demonstrate you or your company as a thought leader in your industry. By posting relevant topics about your industry or sector you will also provide "under the radar selling", which means you can easily bring your products and services into the article in a subtle way, as a solution to the topic that you are writing about.

If you are a retailer, for example, write blog posts about your products. Your customers will get to know you as the knowledge source for the products they want.

If you are in business-to-business (B2B), then post articulate, well-researched articles about your service industry. Become the place to be for your niche market.

Develop better customer relationships

Blogs provide another source to deepen the connection with your customer. By connecting directly on your website, your clients are able to get to know your business or product from the comfort of their computer, smartphone or tablet. Use this. Again, build trust by being a source of information. Consumers like to be informed, and appreciate that you are the one teaching them.

Unlike many social sites, a blog is generally searchable on your site for a long time. Your website comments last longer than a Twitter response or a Facebook post. Other customers will see your interactions too. It is important that you respond, though. If someone posts a comment on your blog, then make sure that you are responding to that comment within a few hours. You want people to feel that you are listening to them, and that you value their contribution.

We recommend a plugin called **https://disqus.com/** for WordPress sites to achieve this. Disqus software has a whole community of its own that is great for stimulating additional interaction and engagement on your website.

As mentioned, a real sin of social media and blogging is to post your blog then have lots of comments, without responding or getting involved. Ensure that you have your notifications set to On, and that you have some type of spam gate that will sift out all the robots that spam your site.

There are many spammers out there and if your website is open, then it is highly probable that they will start leaving random comments on your blog. To spot a spammer, look out for the following:

- They usually start with a compliment of your website or blog, but they never refer to anything specific. For example: "What awesome content! Thank you for providing this great blog."
- The spelling and grammar is usually awful.
- They will always have a link to somewhere in the post.
- Sometimes, they will simply try to sell something, in a similar way to which you receive spam emails.

Place these in the trash, and then signify them as junk, in the same way you would an email.

You are building trust, too. The more you can show that you are well versed in your field, the more likely that your potential customer will trust you to supply what they need.

Do not regurgitate other people's content. Write unique content at all times.

Where to host your blog

There are many popular blogging platforms that you can use. As previously mentioned, it is best to have your blog incorporated into your main website. Alternatively, your blog could be your main website, using a well-known platform called WordPress. Alternative platforms are those such as Tumblr, Typepad, Blogger, etc. But WordPress is by far the most popular, as shown in this infographic by **https://www.wpbeginner.com/beginners-guide/facts-about-wordpress/**

WordPress is not just a blogging platform; it is a complete content management system (CMS) that you can build your whole site on, which obviously incorporates a blog.

Indeed, some of the most famous websites are also built on WordPress. If WordPress is good enough for the Rolling Stones, then it should be good enough for your business, too!

There are two types of WordPress content management systems. See pages 54-55 to ensure you're using the correct platform.

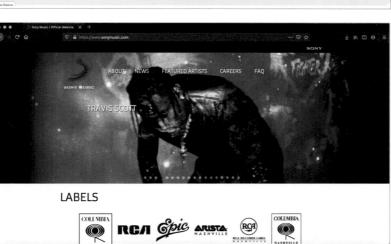

Some other top sites based on WordPress that you may not be aware of are:

- Forbes – **https://www.forbes.com**
- Usain Bolt, the world's fastest man – **http://usainbolt.com/**
- Katy Perry – **https://www.katyperry.com/**

If you are considering using WordPress, then please be aware that there are two types: WordPress.com and WordPress.org. This can be confusing, so we'll show you the pros and cons of each.

...cont'd

There are two main differences between the two sites:

Cost

WordPress.com – This is a free service, and you will have a website address that looks like: "joebloggswebsite.wordpress. com" (this is the same if you are using other free services such as Blogger).

WordPress.org – This is chargeable, and you will have a website address that looks more like: "joebloggs.co.uk" or "joebloggs.com" (there is no mention of WordPress at all, and this is much more professional if you are running a business).

Flexibility

WordPress.com – You are limited to how you can design the site, and the functionality that you can bring to the site.

WordPress.org – You can integrate the site with your email marketing software such as Mailchimp or AWeber, as well as many other applications to make your site funky and marketable.

Sometimes, "free" is not always best. You may think that starting out with a WordPress.com site is a good way to begin, but I would advise jumping in at the deep end, getting yourself a WordPress.org self-hosted site with a professional address (your domain name), and going for it.

Summary of differences:

	WordPress.ORG	WordPress.COM
Is it free?	You can download it for free. However, you will need a domain and hosting, which will incur a cost (usually a low-cost monthly figure).	The basic package is free. But there is a premium package available if you need additional storage.

	WordPress.ORG	WordPress.COM
Setup time	Approximately 15 minutes.	Approximately 5 minutes.
What about plugins and applications?	There are lots, and lots, and lots! At the time of writing this book there were 55,000+ plugins, increasing all the time!	20-30 plugins that are only accessible for premium users.
Can I monetize my site?	If you want, you can monetize your blog and add different adverts. You have complete control and decide which ads go where and how many you would like.	You can elect to run WordAds, which are selected by WordPress and thematically linked to the content of your site, or you can run your own ads.
Updates and maintenance	Updating the blog is your responsibility. It is also highly recommended that you do backups as often as possible. However, updates take a few seconds to complete, and there are plugins to help with backing up your site automatically.	No need to worry. WordPress.com is responsible for your updates and backups.
Storage	Depends on your hosting company. Usually unlimited.	3GB for free (see tip).

WordPress.com comes at different price points to suit the size and requirements of your business. Check out https://wordpress.com/pricing/

Writing the blog post

You have set up your blog, but now what? What on earth do you write about?

One common mistake is people constantly writing about themselves, and what is happening in their business. This is interesting on occasions, but not constantly.

If you are aware of the Pareto Principle (or the 80/20 rule) then the same theory applies to blogging.

80% of your business comes from 20% of your efforts

Therefore 20% of your blog posts should be something to do with your company, your products or services. However, 80% of your posts should incorporate information to do with your industry. They should be topics that are of interest to your visitors.

Some good hooks for you

These are questions that are often asked on email or on the phone. If someone calls and says, "How do you…?", or "I am after some advice, what do you think…?", note these questions down – they will make excellent blog topics.

Your industry will have trade magazines or press articles that will give you some fantastic content ideas for a good blog.

Check out "Today's news and views" on your LinkedIn homepage to find out which topics are hot right now – whilst they might not be directly connected to your business, find the human interest story around the topic and link that to your company, a member of staff, or your customers.

Today's news and views ⓘ

- **Biggest chains test reusable cups**
  1d ago • 11,727 readers
- **Snapchat brings new £20 note to life**
  5h ago • 4,951 readers
- **Laura Ashley grabs funding lifeline**
  12h ago • 11,913 readers
- **Airlines to take a big hit from virus**
  7h ago • 5,117 readers
- **Virus: Deaths outside China rise**
  19h ago • 2,759 readers
- **A much younger boss, does it matter?**
  4h ago • 33,137 readers
- **Youth job aspirations 'mismatched'**
  7h ago • 6,429 readers
- **Are new dads taking parental leave?**
  2d ago • 25,547 readers
- **Is your office vegan friendly?**
  1d ago • 1,318 readers
- **Barclays axes staff spying software**
  10h ago • 543 readers

Show less ∧

If you have a small team of people, then look at some software such as HubSpot's Blog Ideas Generator (**https://www.hubspot.com/blog-topic-generator**), which is a fantastic tool that suggests blog topics for you based on your own choice of keywords.

How does HubSpot's Blog Ideas Generator work?

Simply enter in up to five nouns that are relevant to your business, product or customers, and click Give Me Blog Ideas. The generator will respond with five blog ideas based on your chosen keywords. If you choose to register with HubSpot (it's free) then you can receive 250 blog ideas based on your keywords, downloadable as a spreadsheet.

Consider choosing a theme for your updates for a set time period.

Using Passle is a fabulous way of collecting your blogging ideas.

It's a quick and easy (and cheap!) way to collect ideas for blogs with a touch of a button. By saving the spreadsheet, you can refer back later when you're stuck for fresh ideas. Share the spreadsheet among team members to ensure you will never hit a dry spell for content creation for your site.

...cont'd

Looking for inspiration

Here are some of my favorites from around the web:

Pretty Handy Girl

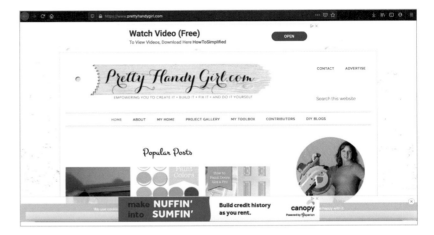

Teach Mama

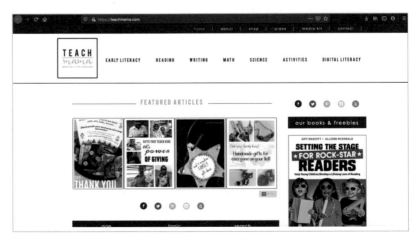

...cont'd

Write to Done

Small Business Trends

Have you included a visual within your blog article?

Is there a process to blogging?

Blogging is an art, and it is important that you have some consistency in the way your blogs look and feel. To make it easy for you, here is a simple checklist for the steps needed to operate a successful blog.

1 Write the blog post

- Does the content show personality and is it conversational?
- Will the readers get value from the article (make sure it is not salesy)?
- Does it answer a question, issue or other topic your readers need or want to know?
- Have you included some type of fact, figure or statistic?
- Use a spell checker.
- Read the article out loud. This is very important, as it is the easiest way to pick up mistakes.
- Ask another person to proofread the article for spelling and grammar.

2 Format your blog post on the website

- Is it easy on the eye? Lists and short paragraphs work really well.
- Headlines from the content – a book called "Advertising Headlines That Make You Rich", by David Garfinkel, has some great ideas.
- Bullets for lists – makes it easy reading for visitors.

3 Tag and hyperlink external and internal sources to further explain points made

To turn a word blue, so that your audience knows that they can click on the word and it will be directed to a website, simply highlight the word with your mouse, and then click **Ctrl** + **K** on a PC or **cmd** + **K** if on a Mac.

Insert Hyperlink

Link to: Paste your website address here...

Display: wordpress

ScreenTip...

Web Page | Document | E-mail Address

Recent Addresses ▶   Launch E-mail Application

To:

Subject:

Enter the e-mail address and subject for messages that will be created when people click on this link.

Cancel   OK

If you are writing your article on WordPress or within an online platform, then look for the hyperlink icon. Then, add your website address.

Highlight your word, then click this link icon

4. Add an image – with a title and an alt description

It is imperative that you are using a copyright-free image, or an image that you have the rights to use. There are numerous places where you can obtain images.

A number of stock images can be found on these sites. However, this is not an exhaustive list:

https://www.dreamstime.com/ – This is the site that we use most often. However, it is a personal choice. Dreamstime offers a range of free images that you can use within your blog, but the best images come with a cost.

https://www.gettyimages.co.uk/ – Getty Images allows you to use any of their images that has the embed facility within your blog, or on social networking platforms, as

...cont'd

long as you are not using the image to promote a product or service for commercial use. They do have certain rules that you need to abide by – see: **https://www. gettyimages.co.uk/company/terms**

https://www.istockphoto.com/

https://www.photos.com/

https://www.shutterstock.com/

⑤ Add a call to action, or an affiliated image

Make the most of each article that you produce by adding a strong call to action. This can be a simple question that you ask – for example:

"Do you have an opinion on XXXX? Please comment in the box below."

Or another option is to have a range of banner adverts designed so that you can change them depending on the content of the blog. Here is a selection of banner adverts that we add at the end of each article:

Once you have added your image, then hyperlink the image (using the same technique as previously mentioned) to the area on your website that gives more detail about the product or service.

6   Add a minimum of four related articles

A little bit like some online stores: you bought this; you may also be interested in these products...

As well as a call to action, add related articles to the bottom of your blog posts so they look like this:

Add related articles

Make sure that at least one of these articles is linked back to a previous article within your OWN website. Google gives you extra points if visitors click within your site, so give them the opportunity to explore.

If you are a WordPress user, then consider using a plugin called Contextual Related Posts: **https://webberzone. com/plugins/contextual-related-posts/**
The plugin allows you to display a list of related posts on your website. The posts selected are based on the content of the title and/or content of the posts, which makes them more relevant and more likely to be of interest to your readers. The best bit? It's completely free of charge!

7   SEO (search engine optimize) your blog post

By now, you can see why it takes approximately one to two hours to create and edit a blog post, but it is worth the investment of time to get it right.

...cont'd

If you are not an SEO expert, it is much easier to add a plugin to your website to ensure that you have ticked all the right boxes for optimizing your website for Google etc. than it is to learn the ins and outs of the fast-changing world of search engine optimization.

There are lots of plugins out there, but Yoast **(https://yoast.com/WordPress/plugins/seo/)** is a plugin that is updated regularly and is really easy to use with its green tick process.

To see if a plugin is a good one or not, check out how many downloads they have on the developer's site, along with the star rating. Here are the statistics for Yoast (*at the time of going to print*):

Get Yoast SEO Premium ▸

Only £79 (ex VAT) for 1 site – including 1 year free updates and support

⬇ Download the free version »

✔ Most downloaded SEO plugin   ✔ Over 135 million downloads   ✔ 4.9 out of 5 stars

Yoast SEO: the #1 WordPress SEO plugin

✔ Get more visitors from Google and Bing
✔ Attract more visitors from social media
✔ Increase your readers' engagement

We walk you through every step: no need to be or hire an SEO expert.

Get Yoast SEO Premium ▸   or   ⬇ download Yoast SEO **Free** »
Only £79 (ex VAT) for 1 site – including 1 year free updates and support

Image source: https://yoast.com/wordpress/plugins/seo/

Here is the checklist for a search engine optimization:

- Title has keyword.
- H tag with the keyword (H tag is a title – i.e. Heading 2, Heading 3 etc.).

Google likes tags. Select H2 or H3 tags for your blog headings/subheadings

- Keyword bolded in content.
- Keyword in the URL/website address (and the URL short and easy to decipher from other content). You can edit the permalink, which changes the URL but does not change the title of the article.
- Appropriate tags.

- Meta keyword – usually 1 or 2.
- Meta description – The meta description is the area that you see in Google that describes the article. Aim for 155-160 characters in length, as Google will truncate any meta description longer than this. If you install a plugin such as Yoast, it is relatively easy to change the meta description by completing a form.

...cont'd

Autocab Technology Platform | Taxi Booking and Dispatch Softwa...
https://www.autocab.com/ ▾
Autocab is the world's leading supplier of private hire **taxi** booking and **taxi dispatch** software
and GPS fleet management systems. 25+ years experience.

This is your meta description

Don't forget

Make sure you have optimized your blog post for search engines.

- Picture alt tagged with the keyword – an "alt tag" or "alternative tag" or sometimes called "alternative description" is a string of words that describes an image on a website. If you hover over an image, then you should see a "pop-up" of a word that has been alt tagged.

So, why use alt tags for your images? The simple answer is that Google can read text, but it cannot read images. Therefore, if you have not alt tagged your images, then Google will see lots of black holes within your website or blog. The other main reason for adding a second title or alternate description is to assist those who are visually impaired. If a user has the Accessibility function enabled on their computer, then when you hover over a tagged image, the computer will read the description out loud.

Caption	How to block someone on LinkedIn
Alternative Text	How to block someone on LinkedIn

 8 ## Publish and distribute your post

If you are feeling creative, then you may want to write a number of posts in one day and then schedule them throughout the week or month. Most blogging platforms will have a scheduling facility.

The process for distribution of blog is an automated process. Those who have subscribed to the blog receive new blogs into their inbox at a set time. **Mailchimp** is an excellent tool for publishing and distributing posts.

Using evergreen content to republish

If at all possible, try to make some of the content on your blog "evergreen". This simply means that it is not date- or time-sensitive, so that you can publicize the content more than once on your different social networking sites.

In the early days of blogging, I would write a blog post for "What is new in social media this week", along with a video that I had created. Not only was it very time consuming to source the information needed, it also took about three to four hours to write the content, put the video together, upload to YouTube and then embed into my website. The content always had lots of hits, but it only had a lifeline of about two weeks and then it became irrelevant.

I learned the hard way, and I now try to only publish content that is evergreen. This way, the content I create has longevity far beyond a few weeks or months.

In the example below, at Autocab we use evergreen content but have gone one step further by categorizing the blog posts based on our customers' major business pain points – allowing visitors to pinpoint their business challenges and find answers quicker.

Timing, style & frequency

Timing

When you post your blog is important. The perfect timing will depend on your audience. Ideally, you want to find the time of day when your potential customers are most likely to read and share your content. This is going to be a time when they're active (most likely during office hours if you offer a service), but not so active that your message is lost among the noise. Try experimenting with different times of day until you get a feel for what that "optimal" time is for you.

Style

Blogs afford you an opportunity to step outside the bounds of the heavily vetted copy on the rest of your site and really develop your company's unique brand voice. Take advantage of that opportunity, and don't be afraid to show the world who you are. Raise that brand flag with pride! Experiment with language and don't forget to add some humor, especially if all the other companies operating in your space tend to produce the same old bland copy.

Frequency

The only thing worse than never blogging at all is starting to and not maintaining the effort. As a visitor to a company's blog, it is disheartening to see that the most recent post is from several months (or years) ago! Perhaps you only do a monthly industry roundup. That's cool. Just stick to it!

Hot tip

Try writing a blog post in the style of your favorite newspaper or magazine.

Guest writers on your blog

There are benefits to being a guest writer on another website, but there are also some excellent benefits to having a number of regular guest bloggers on your own blog. Here are five reasons why you should consider having a guest blogger on a website:

Keeps your blog active

Unless you have a big team, it is very difficult to keep up with content on a regular basis. Consistent frequency is the key to any marketing strategy, and blogging is no different. If you produce an article a week for a month, and then produce zero for the next month, then you will have a negative impact on your search engine results, and your audience will not know when to expect information from you. More people are likely to unsubscribe to your blog if you are not consistent. Having regular guest bloggers on your site is a great way to maintain a consistent frequency.

Builds relationships

As with writing for other blogs, allowing guest posts on your own blog opens the door to building relationships with others in your industry. Networking is almost always a good thing, and it might just lead to profitable joint ventures down the road – you never know!

Increases traffic

If your guest blogger has a fan base, more than likely they'll come along for the ride when their article is published on your blog. The result is more traffic for your blog, and more exposure for you and your business. In addition, you could suggest that your guest blogger actually records themselves reading the article, which you can then produce as an audio blog. You will be surprised how many people are up for this challenge, and how much they will share the content with their own audience if they can also hear themselves, rather than just reading an article.

More content variety

With guest posts, you'll inject your blog with a bit of variety, which most of your readers will welcome. Different authors mean different topics, different perspectives, and different writing styles, all of which can keep your blog from becoming predictable and stale.

Increases guest blogging opportunities for you

Guest writers may return the favor and ask you to guest post on their blog. Take them up on their offer. You can benefit from the wider audience, increased traffic, and a boost in reputation.

Ask others to guest blog on your website. Make sure that the content is unique by checking the content on **grammarly. com**'s plagiarism detector.

Set some rules for your bloggers so it is clear what is expected from them.

Record an audio version of each blog article to help increase your traffic and improve accessibility of your website.

Conclusion

The four steps to online marketing success for blogging:

 Build your platform

Have you built your blog correctly? Do you have keywords in your articles? Is it optimized for search engines? Are you adding images and calls to action to your articles?

If your site is looking good, and indexed correctly, with regular content, then you have reached stage one of success for blogging.

2 Grow your network

Are your comments active? Do you have regular visitors? Do you have those all-important social sharing tools that will help grow your network? Do you have guest bloggers contributing to your site?

If you are growing your network, then congratulations – you have achieved the second stage of blogging success!

3 Create your strategy

Have you decided on how many posts to create each week/month? We recommend at least once every two weeks, keeping the Google spiders happy. Are you consistently producing articles? Are your response times quick on your blogging comments? Have you got a strategy for word count? Have you got a strategy for content topics? Have you set rules for your guest bloggers and given them allocated dates for them to send you content? Have you got a bank of calls to action ready to add to the bottom of your articles?

If you can answer yes to most of these questions, then you have accomplished stage three of your blogging success.

4 Measure the results

When it comes to measuring the results for your blog, you first need to see if your articles are pulling in traffic to your website. This can be achieved by looking at your Google Analytics (covered in Chapter 15).

Other measurements include recording how many people are actually sharing your articles to their network, along with the volume of comments that you may (or may not) be receiving online on the various social networking channels and on the blog itself. I would highly recommend a tool called **https://www.wiselytics.com/**, which provides key metrics you can track including reach, engagement, interactions, and virality, with attention to which social media posts on Facebook and Twitter reached the most fans or had the most visibility.

If you are measuring the results, and tweaking your strategies to better those results, then congratulations! You are now a fully-fledged blogger.

Checklist

How did you score on the 10-point checklist for your blog?

1 Do you have a unique URL/website address for each blog?

2 Are visitors able to leave a comment on your blog?

3 Is your blog easy on the eye?

4 Have you spellchecked your blog?

5 Are your visitors able to easily share your content with their audience? (i.e. Do you have social media sharing tools incorporated within the blog?)

6 Do you have a call to action at the end of your articles?

7 Have you added "related articles" at the end of your blog to encourage readers to explore your site?

8 Have you optimized your blog post for Google? (i.e. included a meta description, added tags and links within the article.)

9 Is ALL of your blog content original and unique? (i.e. the content is not regurgitated from another website.)

10 Are you producing evergreen content?

4 SEM & SEO

What is SEM?

Search engine marketing (SEM) – also known as PPC (pay-per-click) marketing – is a form of online advertising in which advertisers accrue costs when users click their ads. Advertisers bid on the perceived value of a click in relation to the keywords, platforms, and audience type in which it originates.

The basics
SEM is used for all types of campaign goals, including:

- Increasing sales
- Generating leads
- Promoting brand awareness

SEM is all about relevance. Users are searching for specific products, services, and information at any given time. Advertisers have the ability to show a targeted ad at the exact moment this search is occurring. For example, if a user searches for "black shoes", an advertiser can show an ad that exactly relates to "black shoes".

It will take some time to find which campaigns work for you – experiment with small budgets.

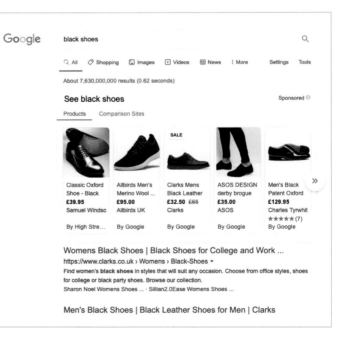

Through both targeting settings and account structure, advertisers can run successful SEM campaigns as long as relevance is paramount. Let's take a look at the two major platforms:

Google Ads

Run on Google, search partner sites, and Display Network sites (see page 80), Google Ads is the largest pay-per-click (PPC) platform. Google Ads was first launched in October 2000 and has gone through several iterations over the last 20 years. Google Ads is geared toward the entire spectrum of companies, from small businesses to Fortune 500.

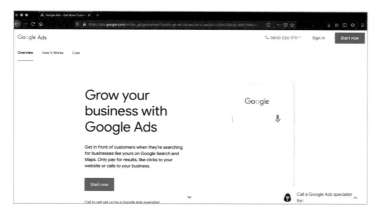

Look at employing a search engine marketing agency to get your campaigns up and running so you can understand how it works.

Microsoft Advertising

Similar to Google Ads, Microsoft Advertising is a pay-per-click platform showing ads on the Microsoft and Yahoo networks. The platform also utilizes search partners. Microsoft Advertising is primarily keyword-based advertising. As of January 2020, Microsoft Advertising had 116 million unique desktop searchers on the Microsoft Search Network*.

*Data taken from **https://about.ads.microsoft.com/en-us**

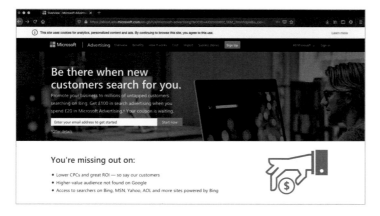

Account structure

Campaigns & ad groups

Advertisers begin by choosing keyword themes and creating individual campaigns. For example, an SEM professional may create a campaign with the theme "Coffee Tables". Within this campaign are themed subcategories, called ad groups. These ad groups may include:

Oval Coffee Tables

Long Coffee Tables

Round Coffee Tables

Each ad group then contains themed keyword variations. For example, the "Oval Coffee Tables" ad group may contain these keywords:

Oval coffee tables

Coffee tables oval

Oval coffee tables on sale

Keywords

Every keyword must be assigned a match type, which defines the queries for which ads will show. There are seven keyword match types:

Exact – Query must be typed in exactly.

Exact (Close Variant) – Query must be typed in exactly, but can include misspellings or other variants.

Phrase – Query must be typed in the correct order, even if there are additional terms before or after the query.

Phrase (Close Variant) – Query must be typed in the correct order, even if there are additional terms before or after the query. Query can include misspellings or other variants.

Broad – Query can be typed in any order and will potentially show ads for similar searches.

Modified Broad – Query can be typed in any order, but must include terms that contain a plus sign.

Keyword research is critical – allocate a whole day to defining keywords that incorporate your brand, product and service.

Broad (Session-Based) – A form of broad match that takes into account other queries from that user's search session.

Here is a table of the match types, keywords, and potential search queries:

Match Type	Keyword	Potential Search Query
Exact	[coffee tables]	coffee tables
Exact (Close Variant)	[coffee tables]	coffe tables
Phrase	"coffee tables"	coffee tables for sale
Phrase (Close Variant)	"coffee tables"	coffe tables on sale
Broad	coffee tables	coffee stands
Modified Broad	+coffee +tables	tables for coffee
Broad (Session-Based)	coffee tables	leather ottomans

Negative keywords
Along with the positive terms, negative keywords can be added to help remove unqualified traffic. For example, someone who searches for "free coffee table" isn't looking to buy. By adding "free" as a negative keyword, the advertiser's ad will not show when a query containing this term is typed. For a company selling high-end products, "bargain" or "cheap" related terms may make good negative keywords.

Audiences
Audiences are groups of users segmented in a variety of ways. Most often, audiences are used in remarketing. Audiences can be created based upon specific page views, time spent on site, pages per visit, and more. Similar to keywords, audiences are bid upon based on relevance. For example, advertisers may bid more to remarket to shopping cart abandoners versus homepage viewers.

Hot tip

Keyword research is an ongoing activity – after your campaigns are running, look to see which words you can add or remove to improve click-through rates (CTRs).

77

Ad copy

Expanded text ads

Once ad groups are created and the keywords chosen, ads can be written. Ads should include the targeted keyword theme, any value propositions, and a call to action (see page 133).

Google Ads' text ad structure and character limits are as follows:

Headline 1 – Up to 30 characters (including spaces).

Headline 2 – Up to 30 characters (including spaces).

Description Line – Up to 80 characters (including spaces).

Path 1 – Up to 15 characters.

Path 2 – Up to 15 characters.

Ads cannot contain excessive capitalization, punctuation, or misleading statements. Keep in mind that the display URL will combine the root of the final URL with Path 1 and Path 2.

It should be noted that expanded text ads replaced traditional text ads in both Microsoft and Google. While still currently eligible to serve within Google Ads, advertisers can no longer create new variations of the traditional ad format. For reference, this consisted of a 25-character headline and a pair of 35-character description lines.

Every ad group should contain at least two ads for testing purposes. Here is an example of an Autocab ad to promote taxi dispatch software:

> **Best-selling dispatch software | Automate your bookings**
> [Ad] www.autocab.com
> join over 110,000 vehicles

Here is an example of the mobile version of the same ad:

> **Best-selling dispatch software | Automate your bookings | Apps that drivers love** ⓘ
> [Ad] www.autocab.com
>
> join over 110,000 vehicles

Don't forget

More visitors now access the web via mobile and tablet devices than desktop devices – always check how your ads display on smaller screens.

You'll write one version of the ad copy that will be automatically formatted for both desktop and mobile. When writing your copy be aware that it will show on both desktop and mobile, and make sure the copy works well on both formats.

Upon clicking, visitors should be taken to a page that continues the ad messaging. This is called the landing page, and it should contain a selection of oval coffee tables with messaging around free shipping.

If you run an e-commerce operation, it's essential your products are displayed within Google Shopping.

Product listing ads (PLAs)

Product listing ads are square units used in e-commerce PPC campaigns that contain product titles, images, and prices.

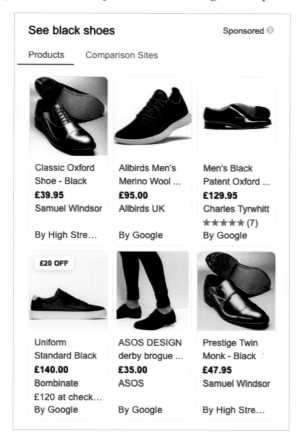

PLAs utilize Google product feeds, and must be connected to a Google Merchant Center account. Microsoft Advertising contains a similar feature called Product Ads.

Campaign types

Search Network – This is the most common targeting option. The Search Network consists of google.com and Google's search partners such as aol.com, amazon.com, and many more. The Search Network is primarily keyword-based advertising. In other words, searchers type in queries for which ads are shown.

Display Network – This network consists of millions of sites that agree to show Google text, image, and video ads. These ads are shown within the site's content and don't utilize traditional keyword-based targeting, but rather audiences and demographics. For example, a user may visit a blog that relates to the history of coffee tables. Even though the user isn't necessarily in a buying mode, the content is relevant to coffee tables. The user may or may not click the ad, but is ultimately now aware of the brand.

Search Network with Display Opt-In – This targeting option is a combination of both networks. In the new Google Ads experience this replaced Search Network with Display Select. Now, you'll create a regular Search Network campaign and opt in to the Display Network. The caveat is that Google determines when and where ads may perform best, taking control away from the advertiser. The preferred option is to break out campaigns by network, but Search Network with Display Opt-In is worth testing.

Shopping: Product Listing Ads – PLAs are shown on Google and Microsoft. After submitting a product feed to Google Merchant Center, shopping campaigns can be created in Google Ads. Advertisers create product groups to which they can bid on various feed attributes. These attributes include:

- Brand
- Category
- Condition
- Item ID
- Product Type
- Custom Attributes

...cont'd

Shopping campaigns do not contain keywords. Both search engines match user queries to the product they deem most relevant. Thus, it is important to ensure all products have accurate information as well as clear titles and descriptions.

Device targeting
Ads can be shown across all devices, including:

- Desktops/laptops
- Tablets
- Mobile devices

Desktops/laptops and tablets are considered similar enough by the search engines that the same bid is applied to these platforms. Mobile devices can have a bid modifier. For example, if the bid is $1.00 and the mobile bid modifier is set to -50%, the bid on mobile devices becomes $0.50. A bid modifier of 150% would set the mobile bid at $1.50.

Location targeting
SEM targeting is extremely granular, going down to the zip/postal code level. Advertisers have many options to ensure that their ads show only in desired locations. The example below showcases a campaign only targeting Iowa.

Hot tip

Location targeting can be as specific as you want – look at creating city-specific ads in which the ad copy is tailored for, say, "Liverpool" or "New York" and see what impact this has on your campaign performance.

Ad scheduling

Advertisers have the ability to run ads only at desired times. Whereas an e-commerce campaign may run ads 24/7, a bricks-and-mortar store may only show ads during business hours. Ad scheduling allows easy management of when ads will show.

Also, just like device and location, bid modifiers can be set for both days and hours. For example, weekends may drive more revenue so bids could be 20% higher on Saturdays and Sundays. Or, poor-quality traffic comes in from midnight to 4 AM so the modifier might be set at -80%.

Budget

Each individual campaign is allowed a daily budget. Budgets should be created in accordance with account goals.

Daily budget	Enter a daily budget $ 50	Your daily budget is the most you're willing to spend each day on your campaign. Actual daily spend may vary ⑦
	Apply from Shared library	
	⌄ Delivery method	

Delivery method

There are two options for which ads are delivered: standard and accelerated. The standard delivery method shows ads evenly throughout the day. This option is good for advertisers who may have budget restrictions and want to ensure their ads show throughout the day. Depending on the budget concerns, ads will not show at all times. The accelerated delivery method shows ads until the budget is depleted. This option is best for advertisers who may not have budget restrictions and want to ensure their ads show for every query.

Ad delivery

There are two options for which your ads will be delivered by Google:

Optimize – Delivery is based upon ads expected to produce higher click volume.

Rotate indefinitely – Ads are delivered more evenly into the ad auction, but they are not optimized toward any kind of goal like clicks or conversions.

Don't forget

Budgets can quickly be used up by broad searches that target too many keywords. The more specific, the better.

Technical SEM

Conversion tracking

Advertisers have the ability to create conversion goals in order to gauge account performance. Both platforms provide code snippets that can be placed on key pages – generally, order confirmation or "thank you" pages. Advertisers are able to determine whether ad clicks are turning into conversions.

Google Ads allows many types of conversion tracking, including:

- Web page.
- Mobile or tablet app.
- Calls from ads using call extensions.
- Calls to a Google forwarding number on your website.
- Clicks on a number on your mobile website.
- Imported goals (from third-party platforms like Salesforce).

Tools

There are a number of tools out there to help you create, manage and monitor your SEM ads. The search engines want to maximize revenue, and thus provide a number of tools to help you manage your campaigns – ultimately hoping that you will increase your spend. Here is a preview of various tools that can support an effective PPC campaign:

Keyword Planner

The Keyword Planner is a tool delivered through Google Ads, which is used to discover and plan your campaigns, keywords, and ad groups. The tool also provides performance data approximations. You can use the data in the Keyword Planner to estimate starting bids and budgets for your PPC accounts.

...cont'd

Audiences

Audiences can be added to Display, Remarketing, and Remarketing Lists for Search Ads campaigns.

Enhanced CPC – A bidding feature where your maximum bid is spontaneously raised for you if Google believes that the click will convert. Your maximum bid using this bid strategy can be up to 30% higher when your ad is competing for a spot on the SERPs. If Google does not think that your ad will convert, then your bid is decreased in the auction. The last part of the Enhanced CPC bidding feature is that your bid will stay at or below the maximum bid you set for certain auctions. Google's algorithms evaluate the data and adjust bids.

Target Search Page Location – This flexible bidding strategy changes bids so your ads can be consistently shown either at the top of the page or on the first page of the SERPs. This strategy is great when your goal is to maximize the number of people who see your ads.

Target CPA – This strategy sets bids to maximize conversions at your target cost per acquisition (CPA). This strategy works well when you want to keep costs down while growing conversions.

Maximize Clicks – A flexible bid strategy that will set bids to help you get as many clicks as possible while maintaining spend. This strategy is useful when click volume is the primary goal.

Target Return on Ad Spend (ROAS) – Some businesses, particularly e-commerce ones, place higher value on certain conversions over others. The target ROAS is a strategy that sets bids to maximize conversions within a target ROAS goal.

Campaign negative keywords

Negative keywords can be managed through the Shared Library, saving time adding negative keywords to multiple campaigns. Most account managers have certain lists of adult terms or industry exclusions that are standard for an account. Maintaining the lists in the Shared Library saves time. The lists can be added account-wide or to selected campaigns in the account.

Campaign placement exclusions

Much like negative keywords, in Display campaigns certain websites convert poorly. Adding a list of campaign placement exclusions will allow the list to be shared across multiple Display campaigns.

Filters

Filters can be created and saved in Google Ads and Microsoft Advertising. They are especially useful when reviewing large campaigns and trying to break them down into more digestible pieces for analysis. You can filter based on all types of performance data and then make bid changes to the filtered group or other actions based on your goals.

Display keywords

Using keywords on the Display Network is called contextual targeting. These keywords match your ads to websites with the same themes. For instance, the Display keyword "shoes" will match to any website that Google deems is related to shoes. These keywords aren't used as literally as search keywords, and they're all considered a broad match. Keywords in an ad group act more like a theme. Display keywords can be used alone, or you can layer them with any other targeting method to decrease scope and increase quality.

Demographics

Demographic targeting allows you to take an audience-centric approach to ad delivery. This allows you to either adjust bidding or limit your audience based on characteristics that can change purchase intent, such as age, gender, parental status, or household income. Gender targeting works similarly to interest targeting. It targets the gender of the user based on information.

Retargeting

The theory of retargeting is that users who have visited your site are both more likely to convert upon visiting again and less likely to click your ad a second time if they aren't already considering converting.

The retargeting code lives under the Shared Library. You'll place that code across all pages of a site, and then set up remarketing lists to target based on which page(s) users did or did not visit, or based on the dates they did or did not visit a page or set of pages.

Retargeting follows your visitors around the web – here is an Autocab advert displaying on a major UK news site

You can create combinations of retargeting lists. For instance, if you have a subscription-based service that needs renewal every 30 days, you could create one list for visitors of your "thank you" page that lasts 30 days and another that lasts 60 days. You could target the one that lasts 60 days while blocking the 30 days one. This would target people who have visited the "thank you" page 30-60 days after that conversion, and you could use ad copy like "time to renew your subscription".

Another classic example of a custom combination is targeting people who have visited the cart of an e-commerce site, while excluding those who have already purchased an item. This strategy allows you to target people who came close to buying, but didn't. They are often persuaded into purchasing with an ad that gives them a bit of a discount or free shipping.

Ad copy for the Display Network will be written similarly to ad copy for the Search Network. It needs to be compelling, have a call to action, and specifically let users know what your product/service is. The more related to your landing page, the better your Display quality score will be.

Don't forget

Visitors aren't always ready to buy the first time they arrive at your website. By using retargeting, you keep your brand and products front-of-mind many days later.

SEO

How does Google search work?
Google is the most-used search engine in the western world. In the UK it has a market share of about 90%; in the USA it has a market share of 93.2%; and as a result, Google has the natural lead on defining which SEO methods are allowed and which aren't.

When you search for a keyword or term on Google, the results are displayed almost instantly, but how does Google find the websites that are relevant, and how does it order the results?

Crawler
The Google spider bot crawls (searches through) billions of web pages every day searching for new and updated content, and it adds some of these pages to its index.

Index
In order for a website to be found through search, Google needs to have it in its index. Google must also add relevant information about the site to its index.

Ranking algorithm
When a search is started, Google looks for results based on a ranking algorithm.

Search engine results pages (SERPs)
Whilst Google's algorithm is a closely guarded secret, Google uses about 200 ranking signals to find the best result in the index for the given query. All the matching results will form the search results list – the SERPs.

Dominating Google SERPs

It's quite common to hear business owners claim they are "number 1 on Google" and for other business owners to desperately *want* to be number 1… but don't limit your ambition. Getting web pages to rank well on page one of Google's search engine results pages (SERPs) is fantastic, but don't be satisfied with one single position on page 1… dominate the page!

I have a very unfortunate name – Jon Smith – I say unfortunate because it's incredibly common, which means from an SEO point of view it is a lot more difficult to rank on Google because it's so common. Think of the millions of web pages out there that mention "Jon", "Smith" or some variant of each.

The more rich content you create, such as videos, images and blog posts, the more chance you have that Google will rank each asset on page 1 of the search results.

But I've used SEO to make sure that pages I own or can influence are ranking well for the search term "Jon Smith", and this means I dominate page 1 of Google. Should I wish, I could also run Google Ad campaigns for my name and take additional places on the page. Imagine this is your brand – there are only 10 spots available and if you are taking up four of them, between SEO and SEM, your competitors will be at a severe disadvantage.

The tenets of good SEO

For successful and sustainable SEO, this is the criteria Google follows:

Help Google to find your website

- Ensure all your pages are discoverable via internal links.
- Use a sitemap.
- Keep the number of internal links to a minimum.
- Use the HTTP header If-Modified-Since.
- Manage the crawling budget (robots.txt).
- Submit the website to Google (search console).

Help Google to understand your website

- Create a helpful and informative website.
- Understand the search intention of your target audience and create content that supports this.
- Use a clear site hierarchy.
- Ensure your CMS is not blocking Google from accessing content.
- Ensure that other assets, such as CSS and JavaScript data, are accessible by Google.
- Reduce the visibility of session IDs and URL parameters for search robots.
- Prevent crawlers from following advertising links with the help of robots.txt or rel="nofollow".

...cont'd

Help the visitor to use the website
- All links should be valid and pointing to live pages.
- Optimize the loading time of the website.
- Make the website compatible for different screen sizes.
- Make the website compatible with different browsers.

Basic principles of the quality guidelines
- Create a website for users, not for search machines.
- Don't create different user/crawler experiences via cloaking (see below).
- Avoid the use of manipulative ranking tricks.
- Create a unique website experience.

Avoid the following methods
- **Link exchange programs** – Websites that encourage you to add various (often random) links to your website in return for links to your website being added to other sites, with the intention of improving your SEO. It simply doesn't work and, in fact, will likely negatively impact your SEO if the Google bot spots the behavior.
- **Cloaking** – Serving a page of HTML text to search engines, while showing a completely different page (typically made up of images or Flash to users) to human visitors.
- **Bridging or doorway pages** – Pages designed to rank well for particular phrases or keywords, which often feature spammy, keyword-stuffed content with little or no user value.
- **Hidden links** – Masking text or links within a web page so that they are hidden to human visitors but visible to the Google bot in a bid to improve SEO; for example, white text on a white background stuffed with keywords.
- **Copied content** – Google values originality, and the bots know if they've seen the same content elsewhere. If you've copied content from another website or a manufacturer's brochure, Google will not rank the page, as it views it as duplicate content.

5 The customer journey

By understanding the customer journey you'll enjoy better results from your digital marketing, by offering just the right content at just the right time.

The customer journey

The buyer or customer journey is your prospects' way to discover your company and product, and pay for your solution. If you can map it, you will be able to acquire many more new customers. Therefore, to really supercharge your digital marketing, it's essential you understand each stage of the customer journey – what prospects require at each of those stages in terms of content to help them make their buying decision, and how you shepherd prospects through each stage by predicting their needs and having the right marketing content available at just the right time.

Don't forget

Visitors will arrive at your website at different stages of the customer journey – the trick is to ensure you have content that fits the stage they are at.

What is a customer journey?
A definition of the customer journey could be summarized as "the numerous touchpoints your prospects have with your brand before they pay you for your solution".

It tells you how many times, where, when and how your clients met with your brand before they became your clients.

The buyer journey, therefore, can be planned, but you shouldn't design it strictly: because your prospects will individually, freely act in it. So, you always have to analyze it and replan your lead generation, user acquisition, and content strategy.

But there are different types of models that try to structure or at least help you find the right strategies and map your business's own buyer journey:

- Easy-to-convince model
- Before-and-after model
- Circular model
- Consistency model

But let's take a well-known model: the inbound buyer journey, because it's easier for everybody to use it for their own industry.

The inbound buyer journey consists of three main stages:

- Awareness
- Consideration
- Decision

Usually, your prospects start with the awareness stage, then they change into the consideration stage, and at the end of the day they buy. But you can find people that are already in the consideration or decision stage: those are the low-hanging fruits you should consider targeting!

Now, let's go stage by stage, explain their meanings and list what you can do in order to increase the efficiency of your digital marketing strategy to maximize sales.

Awareness stage

This stage is the first stage when we talk about the buyer journey, and it is aimed at the people who are far away from buying your product.

There are two main types of people in this stage:

 Your prospects who feel that they have a need, but they don't yet usually know what exactly.

 People who don't even recognize that they have a need.

The importance of the awareness stage varies from industry to industry.

If you are in a market that doesn't exist yet (for example, you are a startup with a disruptive solution that changes the way we think about a specific thing), your main task is to educate people on even the problem you solve/need you fulfill!

On the other hand, if you enter a well-known, matured market, it is possible that you don't need to educate people much to make them understand the challenge (for instance, if you offer a project management tool). But they may not yet know of your existence or what your firm offers above and beyond the competition.

So, your focus on this stage truly needs to be decided based on the type of problem you solve/need you fulfill, and on the market you are in.

It is important to know that the people at this stage usually use search engines to find answers, be it a search on Google or asking questions from more experienced users on trade/industry forums such as LinkedIn groups (see pages 244-245).

They usually try to search for the symptoms and find the root problem: they are educating themselves on the problem and challenges they are facing or will face.

How to target this stage

When prospects start their buyer journeys, the importance of search engines is very high. You have to know that these people will look for short-tail keywords: keywords with one to two words only. These are usually umbrella terms that help them find the components of their challenge.

This is why SEO experts say that the shorter the keyword, the lower the buying intention. For example, a prospect looking for a new CRM system will type something similar to "CRM software".

As a result, the content you are creating for the awareness stage is not to sell your product or service. Whilst this might seem counterintuitive, these prospects simply aren't ready yet for the "hard sell'. The purpose of awareness content is to guide your prospects toward learning more about (and even defining) the problem they face rather than the solution itself.

If you are in a very new market, it means that you have to put in a lot of effort: to make them understand that they have a problem/need and they need a solution. There are not many competitors in the market yet who could educate them… so now they question if it is a must.

Visitors at the awareness stage may not know what business pain they're facing – spell it out.

95

Awareness stage: use content marketing to get noticed and obtain web traffic

The first stage of the buyer's journey involves getting people to see and read your content.

The people you want to attract are looking for answers, so naturally, the kind of content you should provide at this stage must be focused on that. Your goal here is to inform them about their problems/needs and the best ways to solve them, and with a bit of research, you'll be in the best position to address that need.

...cont'd

The relevant types of content for the awareness stage are:

- **Newsletters and email marketing**: Keep in touch regularly with your subscribers with newsletters and email marketing campaigns.
- **White papers**: Pull out all of your expertise and convert this into well-written and compelling white papers.
- **Blog posts**: Blog posts are also helpful at this stage, because they're easily digestible and can be informative at the same time.
- **Checklists and tip sheets**: Other types of content that work well at this stage are checklists and tip sheets.
- **Infographics**: Visual content like infographics is an excellent choice for effective dissemination of information.
- **Social media updates**: You can also use social media updates with links to your content to generate traffic and awareness.

Remember, though, that the ideal approach here is to offer these resources for free. You'd be hard-pressed to find people willing to pay you for information that they can just as easily get anywhere else. Set aside that financial goal for now, and focus on the fact that your objective is to inform and assist, not to make a profit from the get-go.

Of course, as discussed in Chapter 7 – Marketing automation, while you may be giving away valuable content for free, this content will be gated – i.e. ebooks and white papers hidden behind a form. Prospects get value-added information, but in return they identify themselves to you and provide contact information that you can use to follow up with additional information tailored for their stage of the buyer journey.

Consideration stage

Consideration is the stage where your prospects know the problem/need – they are already educated. They managed to clearly define the root causes, so the time has come to look for a solution that is able to satisfy it.

Within mature markets, you will find lots of people – regardless whether it's business-to-business (B2B) or business-to-consumer (B2C) – that are at this stage. They know already that they need a tool to fix the business pain they actually have right now.

So, they tend to search for the solutions. They probably won't go with one solution right away; they find a number of providers operating in the same space and "consider" them against each other, checking their features and offers.

People will continuously choose between the features: this is why your feature set is positioning your product. But your communication also affects it: the brand you build up in prospects' minds will affect much at this stage.

This is the place where you compete with other solutions directly. But the strategy you choose to compete with others is up to you: you can offer a cheaper, better, faster, more modern, very reliable service (and more). Associating these types of values with your brand not only differentiates you from your competitors but also positions your offer in your prospects' minds.

How to target this stage

The consideration stage will define the keyword types, too: the three to four words are usually the search terms that specifically target a well-defined problem. For example, a prospect looking for a new CRM system will now understand what s/he can expect from most CRM systems on the market and what business pains they fix, so will be a little bit more specific – i.e. "CRM software for small teams". So, ranking for these specific keywords with content that answers this specific search will help your firm to be "considered".

But as you might know, solving this specific problem can be achieved in many ways! If a company has a problem with their existing CRM tool, that doesn't mean they will just go with yours because you say it's marvelous for small teams.

Don't forget

Customers at the consideration stage will also be considering your competitors – ensure you highlight your USPs (unique selling propositions).

...cont'd

They will want to know why it's perfect for small teams, and which features, specifically, will make their day-to-day activities easier and more productive. So, you need to argue that your type of solution has the highest potential to satisfy their needs.

In order to do that, you should create in-depth guides, podcasts, and video content to explain the advantages of your type of solution.

But keep in mind that you still don't have to be too pushy with your sales pitches. People are looking for answers to their questions: what is the solution type that solves their problem/need the best?

Beware

If visitors are considering your product or service, then they are going to want to know about your pricing – if you would prefer to keep that hidden for now, ensure they can contact you to request pricing, or you might lose out to those companies that display their pricing clearly.

Consideration stage: develop a content marketing strategy for getting leads and keeping them

I've never met a salesperson, business owner or company executive whose top priority didn't revolve around obtaining leads and sales.

These are the most crucial things at this stage:

● When you reach this part of the B2B buyer's journey, engagement becomes a more critical component.
● You need to infuse your content with opportunities to reach out and engage with your audience on a more personal level.

Companies who rethink their lead generation strategy thoroughly enjoy a significantly higher response rate compared with those who don't – up to 10 times higher.

So, what kind of content should you be putting out at this stage?

The potential buyers at this stage already know what you can offer them to address their pain points – your goal now is to build your credibility further.

The relevant types of content for the consideration stage are:

- **Webinars, live streaming and live events**: These are popular ways to demonstrate your expertise on a particular subject.
- **Case studies**: You can also publish case studies that talk about the benefits that working with you can offer, or even an objective comparison between you and your competitors to show them what makes you unique – and ultimately causes them to select you as a possible solution.
- **Reviews and testimonials**: You can also use reviews and testimonials to demonstrate social proof, enhancing your credibility to potential buyers.
- **Social selling**: You can incorporate social selling at this stage to gain further interest from potential buyers.
- **LinkedIn lead generation**: LinkedIn is also particularly useful at this stage to generate leads.

If you use case studies, check every couple of months that the companies you feature are still using your product/service.

This is the last step in the buyer journey before your prospect pays for your actual solution or service. If they know that your type of solution is good for them, they want to pick one.

This is the place where you face the direct competition: actual features on offer and the price are pitted against each other in a head-to-head comparison.

Decision stage

If your pricing, the features, and everything else fit, you successfully acquire a new customer. But as Lincoln Murphy said, today's prospects don't want solutions. They want to find their "desired outcome": you have to help them get to their desired outcome in an appropriate way.

This is where the overall feeling of your company (not your product) will affect whether you can acquire a new customer at the end of the buyer journey.

So, take it into consideration: using our example earlier of a prospect looking for a new CRM solution for their small team, then bigger brands (like Salesforce, Zoho, and Zendesk) will now acquire clients far easier than a new solution if they would choose the same strategy.

Newer, not well-known brands have a more difficult time when it comes to sales – it is just how things work; sorry. But no worries: a good USP (unique selling proposition) can change that!

It's not just one person in an organization making the buying decision – provide shareable content your lead can distribute within their organization to help the other decision-makers believe in your offering too.

How to target this stage

For this stage, use sales pitches, product videos, comparison pages, testimonials, product-specific case studies, and the offer of a free trial.

If you choose to offer your free trial, the first in-app experience will be one of the most important things: create astonishing user onboarding that truly helps your prospects achieve their success milestones. The faster they reach it, the higher the possibility that they will pay.

Also, it is important that you "activate" your trial users and keep them engaged.

Activation mainly helps them in taking action and feeling the power of your tool. Keeping them engaged relies on your product and whether you are able to surprise and delight them. If you make your prospect smile just for a second, you will be closer to your goal.

You can also offer consultations and educative content to help them get started as fast as it is possible.

If you offer a free trial, contact the customer during the trial period to assess their adoption of your product – don't wait until the trial ends.

SWOT ANALYSIS

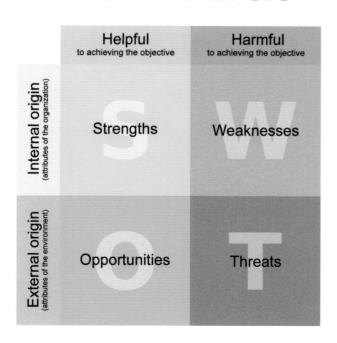

...cont'd

The decision stage: focus your content strategy on getting sales

This is the selling point – the part you've been carefully building up to with all your content offers. If you set things up in the earlier stages, you should be reaping the benefits now.

One thing to remember is that you have to be patient. In this stage, all of those offers can be put to good use. The relevant types of content for the decision stage are:

- **Free trial, consultations, assessment, quotes/proposals, and demos**: You can share free trials and demos with your buyers, invite them to request a quote from you, or even offer free consultations to get them moving along on their journey.
- **Sales conversation**: At this stage, you can also get on the phone or meet in person to have a conversation to discuss how your solution will solve the buyer's problem/need and increase their confidence in your product or service.

Don't forget

Although you might operate an inside sales function, for larger clients consider offering a physical meeting or video conference with their stakeholders to show how important their business is to your organization.

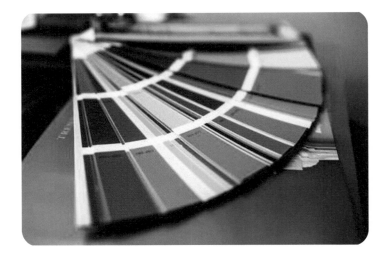

Customer success stages

In addition to the three stages mentioned previously, if you want to keep your customers there are two extra stages that are important: the retention stage and the evangelist stage. The retention stage focuses on the customer's impression of your product and what type of messages you are sending to them. The evangelist stage is about the advocates of your brand and your communication toward them.

The retention stage: incorporate retention and referrals into your content marketing strategy

After making a sale, don't leave your customer behind. This is the stage where you need to be present for them. This is the perfect time to make them feel that they are an important part of your community.

The relevant types of content for the retention stage are:

- **Email marketing**: Implement email campaigns that get them acquainted with your other products and continue to educate and nurture them.
- **Social media updates**: Develop a consistent social media management strategy.
- **Live streaming and videos**: Send them emails announcing when you're doing some live streaming or you've uploaded a new video.
- **Blog posts**: Publish a new blog post at least once a week.
- **Case studies**: Organize case studies and make sure they are up-to-date.
- **Podcasts**: Podcasts are also a great way to create a voice for your brand that your customers can listen to.

It's far cheaper to retain customers than generate new business. Listen to customer concerns and put as much effort into retention as you do into new business development.

...cont'd

The advocacy stage: develop your loyal customers into brand advocates

To get repeat business, nothing beats the magic of referrals.

To gain advocates for your brand, these are relevant types of content for the advocacy stage:

Advocates will tell their network about their experience with your product or service – treat them like VIPs and they will supercharge your marketing efforts.

- **Warm introductions and referrals**: Maintain relationships with your customers and notice who they are connected to. The third-party credibility you get from receiving a warm introduction goes a long way in accelerating the sales process.
- **Social media engagement**: Watch what your customers and prospects post online – don't miss an opportunity to like, comment or share their posts when relevant.
- **Social sharing of content**: Make sure that your content is easily shareable. Add social sharing options to your website and all other content.
- **Webinars**: Continue to add value to your existing customers by offering an educational webinar series and allow them to invite others to it.

6 Customer profiling

Your customers are unique. No two people think and act the same. By profiling your customers you can create customer types, and tailor your digital marketing to appeal to specific profiles – leading to more successful campaigns and a better return on investment (ROI).

What is customer profiling?

Customer profiling is basically collecting details about customer demographic criteria – i.e. personal interests/hobbies. This information is used in marketing to understand customers better, in order to make more targeted advertising and promotional material.

Traditionally, a customer profile only consists of basic information such as their age, location, marital status, income range, etc. Today, more complex strategies and sophisticated techniques are being used, like mining data from many databases. It's a way of identifying meaningful patterns to produce more useful segmentation, even in large groups of customers.

Getting specific

You may already have a sense of who your customers are. This sense can be derived from a whole cloud of resources including news articles, secondary research into markets and trends, observations and experiences, conversations and, most commonly, assumptions.

It is fine to use assumptions and biases as starting points to define who your customers are, but it is dangerous not to challenge them. Customer profiling uses these assumptions positively as starting points to help create a specific picture of one single fictional user, buyer, partner or investor. It then imagines how they live, what they prefer, how they like to be communicated with and, ultimately, how they would relate to your product or service.

By going deep into detail, you build on what is known and what is assumed, and show the value of qualitative customer research alongside the quantitative. There is no substitute for speaking with real people, but customer profiling is a valuable first step in defining criteria to seek out customers (or potential customers) to participate in feedback, co-creating ideas and solutions, prototyping, or focus groups. This in turn can lead to you creating better products and services that truly meet the needs of your customers.

Developing customer profiles

Start by creating a detailed picture – a customer persona – of someone you want to connect with. It's absolutely fine to pick one specific person – you can run this exercise again for different users representative of different groups, and even markets. As you flesh out their profiles, consider the decisions you make about who you are prioritizing and why. Ideas for more profiles that are representative of other customer groups and sub-groups will emerge. Make a note of them for later, and avoid diluting who you're working on right now.

Your customer persona will become more specific as you move from demographics such as age, gender, income, and location to include more aspirational, behavioral, and psychographic qualities. It can be unnerving to put so much imagination into a persona, but it actually improves their tangibility, allowing you to empathize with, relate to, and query them, and could surface questions you may not have considered.

Building an ideal customer profile really isn't that complicated but you'll definitely benefit greatly from external expertise. Developing the best customer profile begins with three essential steps:

There is no right or wrong answer in terms of how many customer profiles you should create. As a starting point, try to create five.

1 **Analyzing the market** – The first step to creating a customer profile is to analyze your market. What does the competitor's customer look like? What do typical customers in the market usually look like? How do they behave currently and how have they behaved in the past?

2 **Use third-party data** – Using third-party data enriches your information and increases your demographics. It will also show connections in relationship information, showing the hidden opportunities of cross-selling and up-selling. Don't miss adding more information that could help in enriching your customers' profiles and maximizing the value of your existing data. The corporate family linkage may also give your profiling added value, for it shows relationships and connections between different companies.

...cont'd

Hot tip

Measure not just the value of a customer's individual basket or product purchase, but their value to you over 12, 24 and 36 months – this will give you their Lifetime Value (LTV) and can help you further profile "big" one-off purchase customers and repeat customers who may buy small but often, and can be worth a lot more to your business over the long term.

3 **Apply marketing analytics** — Applying analytics in your customer profile can give you the kind of quality customers that are very valuable to your business. It can also help you predict future behavior. Usually, customers are ranked according to their response rate or purchase history. A baseline is then created to determine the standard of the "most valuable" type of customer and will serve as the "model customer" in segmenting your data according to each customer's value. In customizing scores based on your information, you may do the following:

● Choose the best model.

● Segment your prospects based on their similarity to the model customer.

● Estimate demand (the revenue potential the best customer can offer).

● Eliminate low-potential customers.

What to include

The most typical and effective customer profile must cover a combination of two important factors: the demographics and the psychographics.

Demographics – quantifiable characteristics of your prospective customers, such as their:

● Gender.

● Age.

● Physical characteristics (body type, hairstyle).

● Hometown/neighborhood.

● Race/ethnicity.

● Education level.

- Occupation.

- Household.

- Living situation.

- Religion.

Psychographics – psychological or mental characteristics, interests, and beliefs:

- Likes/dislikes.

- Hobbies.

- Favorite TV shows, music, websites, or other media.

- Interests.

- Political views.

- Anxieties.

- Spending habits.

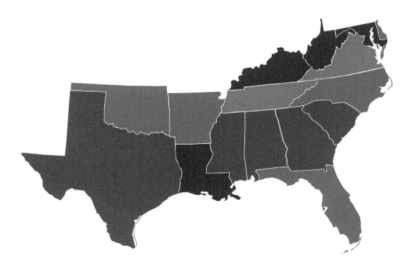

...cont'd

Depending on the product or service you provide, you may feel that some of these profile items are irrelevant. Choose what you think you should capture and add topics that are relevant to your business.

Key demographics to focus on

Age – Taking the age factor into consideration is the first and the most important step of customer profiling. It is based on the belief that a consumer's needs and desires change as they age. For example, a well-known skincare brand, Olay, has attempted to shrug off its competitors by targeting middle-aged women.

Furthermore, in the advertisement of Torex Cough Syrup, the scene is directly communicating with older people. As a cough-relief product, it can be expected to have more demand in such age groups.

Gender – Gender can give a good indication of interest in a product or service. Although not an exact science, product teams will decide early on if they're designing a product for men, women or both. This will impact the product design but also, potentially, the entire advertising campaign. Who's buying your product or service? Can you tailor messages to focus on one gender? And crucially, should you?

110

Hot tip

Although your product or service may be designed with a specific age demographic in mind, the market can often surprise you. Look for indicators that another demographic is purchasing, and if the sales numbers look good, look to create new packaging and marketing to grow sales to that profile.

Income – Mercedes, Ferrari, BMW: all these cars have customers that are much more quality- and luxury-conscious than the users of lower-income car brands. Of course, the customers with a higher income would be the target group of such products. Similarly, in fast-moving consumer goods (FMCG) you will see many brands and products that are targeted toward a different section of customers. These customers are divided on the basis of their income and purchasing power.

Education – The level of education an individual has had greatly influences his/her buying decisions. If your product or service has much to do with knowledge, your target audience group will relate to highly educated people. As an example, a product like "Intel core processor" has a clear target of a higher-educated audience.

Moreover, education and income are correlated. The more educated a person is, the greater the income s/he earns, thus the more will be their purchasing power. Also, consider whether they are urban or rural as this again helps define their education level.

Occupation – What occupation do most of your customers hold? Is their occupation a major issue? Professional managers, business owners, craftspeople, farmers, homemakers, the unemployed, the retired masses, and students are examples of major categories of various targeted customer profiles based on occupation. Ideally, a company CEO will buy luxury cars and subscribe to a golf club membership. Similarly, a teacher will purchase books, papers and pencils, as well as other such lower-priced products.

Effectively employing the power of the above-stated demographics makes it possible to successfully conduct customer profiling, which plays a crucial role in understanding the customer needs and popular market trends to give your digital marketing strategy the very best chance of success.

...cont'd

Hot tip

Revisit your customer profiles regularly – send questionnaires to existing customers and check that your profiles truly reflect the customers you have.

The end result

When using this information to take action, the data from your customer profiles is a major factor in increasing your profitability or return on investment (ROI). The success of your lead generation will rely on your understanding of the profiles of your customers. Building an ideal customer profile is every business's weapon in generating leads, turning your leads into sales, having customers returning for more, and, most importantly, improving your marketing ROI.

7 Marketing automation

By automating much of your marketing you can streamline your business development, communicate with the right customer at just the right time, and improve your conversion rates – leading to more customers and more profits.

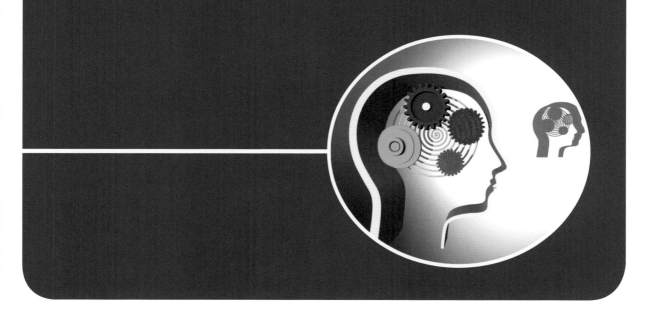

Marketing automation

Chances are, you've heard the term "marketing automation" before, but perhaps you haven't really dug into what it actually means – and that's OK!

Marketing automation, put simply, refers to software that exists with the goal of executing marketing actions (e.g. publishing social media posts, sending out emails, and so on) without any manual effort.

This software, when used correctly, nurtures prospects with helpful (and personalized) content that is meant to convert them into loyal customers.

Why use it?

Marketing automation saves time (and money). Here are some incredible takeaways:

- When you automate your social posts and ads, on average you save more than six hours per week.
- You can increase your reply rate by 250% by automating your outreach and follow-up emails.
- You can save 80% more time by setting client appointments or meetings with an automated tool.

No longer do you have to go into a tool every morning and schedule your social media posts for the day or ship one-off emails. Thanks to marketing automation, you can schedule everything you need ahead of time, which will free you up to do other marketing activities. Who doesn't like to "set it and forget it"?

More than that, all-in-one marketing automation tools such as Pardot, HubSpot, and – in the UK – Force24 will save you time jumping from platform to platform. When you're constantly flipping between tabs just to get a campaign in motion, you waste a lot more time than you'd think.

"Big picture" data

Marketing automation software allows you to tag all of your marketing activities with the campaign they're associated with, and also see comprehensive analytics of your traffic, conversion rates, clicks, etc. all in one place. Robust, multi-functional tools like this give you a big picture of your data and how everything works together, rather than forcing you to jump from platform to platform.

Even more, you can access reports and look at how everything is performing in real time.

When using one tool specifically designed to track how your marketing efforts are affecting your sales, you get the visibility you need to pivot your strategy immediately. Red flags (and general poor performance) won't come as a surprise.

Consistency

With a marketing automation tool, you can rest easy knowing that your online audience will receive the same and consistent experience based on their actions.

When a user subscribes to your blog, for example, you can set up a workflow that automatically sends a welcome email suggesting articles and perhaps sharing a follow-up offer. Depending on your blog setup, you can then also have your new articles automatically sent to subscribers as they are published.

With marketing automation, this is all done on its own; no need to worry about manually sending out emails to your database.

Hot tip

Before starting your marketing automation planning, be sure to check out Chapter 6 – Customer profiling.

Enabling personalization

This ensures that no matter when a user jumps into a workflow, they'll always get optimized messaging.

Through marketing automation software you can add personalization tokens (such as the recipient's name) into an email blast. Incorporating elements like these makes your emails appear more personal, as if they were sent specifically to them rather than to a large list.

When a contact receives an email that looks as though it was personalized for them, they'll be more likely to open it and engage.

Think about it this way – would you be more likely to click through a general newsletter or an email that looks as though it was meant just for you, with your name and a line of text saying "We thought you'd be interested in X, Y, and Z because we noticed you downloaded Offer #1!"?

I think it's safe to say we'd all go for the latter!

With marketing automation, these personalized workflows are easy to set up, and deliver incredible results. It's all about reaching the right person at the right time with the right message. It's about customizing your content to meet your personas' needs and/or provide the solutions they're looking for when they need them.

Marketing automation lets you create a more systematic approach to marketing that you can track and monitor. When you use an all-in-one tool such as HubSpot, you get full visibility into your efforts as a whole and, even more, how your efforts are paying off. It allows you to easily attract new users, convert them into leads, and nurture them through the sales funnel. There aren't any surprises along the way or contacts being lost without you realizing it.

With automation, business owners are finding they can take their marketing to a more data-driven and scalable approach.

Don't forget

To fully enjoy the benefits of marketing automation, choose a solution that integrates with your CRM system so you can easily mail segments of your database with your latest content.

Accelerating acquisition

Your prospects will engage with your content as they progress along the customer journey (see Chapter 5) but one of the most important challenges is to shorten your company's sales cycle. So, you need to softly urge your customers by guiding them through your marketing funnel and giving them the right content, at the right time.

This is why lead generation is so important. If you can catch your prospects' email addresses, you will be able to send them emails, segmenting them according to the stages of their customer journey and according to their buyer persona.

For example, if you see that a subscriber read one (or more) pieces of content that is relevant to the consideration stage, you can offer him/her a decision-stage content (for example, offering your trial) by sending automated, personalized emails. It is a very effective way of nurturing your leads and helping them get to the bottom of your funnel faster.

Personalized messaging means personalized content too. It means that you shouldn't send a person content that is not relevant to her/his stage.

Beginning at lead generation and ending at sales, lead nurturing describes everything you do in between these two stages to earn a customer: writing blog posts, tweeting, calling on the phone, etc.

Check out your competitors' content marketing to generate new ideas for your own ebooks and articles.

Although you will lose leads at each stage of the funnel, the more quality leads you feed into the top, the more likely it is that you'll have a significant number converting into customers.

Nurturing leads – dos/don'ts

As important as it is to know how to nurture leads, it's just as important to know how to avoid losing them. Just one poorly written ebook, email, or tweet could mean the difference between keeping leads in your funnel for another round of marketing, and forcing them out. Think you know what it takes to turn prospects to customers? Find out:

Do: establish a definition of qualified leads

Nurturing leads successfully means that, at some point, the sales team will take over the marketing. This happens, usually, toward the bottom of the funnel (but it can vary from team to team). And when it happens, it's important that the marketing team hands off qualified leads to sales.

Leads are qualified if they're more likely to purchase based on their behavior throughout the funnel. And that behavior varies from business to business.

For example, downloading certain white papers or attending specific webinars might be actions historically taken by leads who go on to buy. People who spend a certain amount of time on a pricing page and return to that page several times over the course of a day or two may be displaying a sense of urgency.

Some organizations ask "Would you like to be contacted by sales?" on their registration forms to make it easy for a lead to self-identify as ready and willing to talk to sales right now.

Audit your funnel, your assets, and your CRM (customer relationship management) data. Start with your best customers and discover what path they took to purchase. Then, reshape your marketing initiatives based on it.

Do: use analytics to turn leads to customers

If you're a SaaS (software as a service) business selling a digital product, and you offer a free trial of your service, the right kind of nurturing can turn leads to paid customers. Like you would use analytics to determine a qualified lead, you can do the same to nudge leads toward buying.

At Autocab we review our new business sales over the previous six months to discover features and activities that lead to purchase. Then, we use these insights to create an onboarding journey that compels visitors to take part in the activities and use the features that improve the likelihood of them buying.

Also, we have casual conversations with new sign-ups. By talking to subscribers in person, through follow-ups, and in in-app and Net Promoter Surveys (NPS), we're able to validate our quantitative assumptions.

Early on, one of our biggest discoveries was that offering a demo too early was detrimental to sales performance – those leads who spent a little bit more time in the consideration stage consuming case studies, watching video testimonials, and had a better understanding of which business pains our software fixed, were five times more likely to purchase after the demo, having already understood what our software can do.

Going forward, the marketing team compelled users to research our USPs (unique selling propositions) and learn how we had solved challenges for similar companies first before demonstrating how it could help their business. By working backwards from your ideal client, you'll be able to discover similar triggers like these that lead to sales.

Use Google Analytics to measure the impact of your marketing automation – find out more in Chapter 15.

...cont'd

Do: create content for every stage of the customer journey

It's been reported that prospects will navigate around 70% of the customer journey without you. So, how does a business help potential customers through it without contacting them?

With content.

From the top of the funnel to the bottom, you should have content for all your buyer personas. Who are they? What will they need to know about you to make a purchase decision?

The types of content you'll create for each stage and each persona will vary, but this graphic from HubSpot offers a good starting point:

Don't forget

One piece of content – say, an ebook – can be cut and reworked into a number of social posts, blogs, articles and infographics.

This is content that's easy to access and easy to consume. If it's gated, a post-click landing page form rarely requires more than a name and email address for access. It also focuses on broader educational topics like "lead-nurturing dos and don'ts", for example, and less on product-related ones. This content should be thought of as "getting to know you" content for the prospect. It's what visitors peruse, usually, long before they're ready to buy (though that doesn't mean they won't read it after).

In the middle of the funnel is interest content. From the prospect's perspective, this is "getting to like you" content. They've read some of your ebooks and attended a webinar or two, and they've decided your kind of product might be what they need to overcome their business issues.

These longer-form content pieces will occupy your leads with more complex topics and, in some cases, more information about you. Case studies can prove what's capable with your solution; reports can establish you as an authority. Lead-capture post-click landing pages can work at every stage to capture new, additional lead information, which helps you further qualify potential buyers as they progress through the funnel.

If and when they're ready, content in the purchase stage is all about you. From a business standpoint, this is "getting to hope you like me" content. By this time, you've offered blog posts, white papers, tip sheets, frequently asked questions (FAQs), and more for next to nothing in return. Content in the purchase stage is about you… of course, with the ultimate goal of informing them about features and capabilities, use cases, etc.

This content will ultimately provide your visitors with the rest of what they need to know. Here, they decide whether or not to pull out their credit card. With a robust content marketing funnel, you'll greatly boost the chances they do.

Purchase a subscription to an image library such as Adobe Stock or Shutterstock to bring your content to life with fantastic visuals.

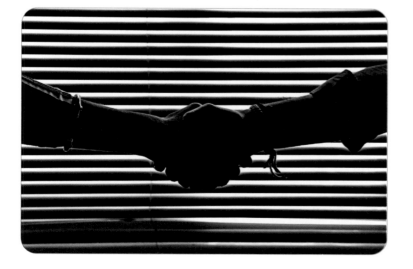

...cont'd

Do: nurture with gated landing pages

At every stage of the funnel, qualifying leads is about learning more about them. Who are these anonymous website visitors? And, are they serious about your product or service? With analytics, you can track behavioral indicators, but when it comes to self-reported information, there's no better tool for learning about your visitors than specific landing pages.

Landing pages are stand-alone web pages created strictly to convert visitors. Whether the goal is to sign up, download, subscribe, or any other action, these pages use uniquely persuasive elements to do it. There are many types of landing pages, and each excels in a different part of the marketing funnel at qualifying your leads for nurturing:

- Short-form pages work at the top of the funnel to capture the minimum amount of information needed to begin the nurturing process. Usually, that's at least an email address and no more than name and email address, in exchange for an asset like a regular newsletter, a tip sheet, or an ebook.

- Lead-capture gated landing pages work at all stages of the funnel to capture as little or as much information that you need at a particular stage. They request personal information through a lead capture form in exchange for a gated asset.

- Ebook gated landing pages work well at the top of the funnel. They capture information in exchange for an ebook – a highly popular top-funnel asset for its value and ease of consumption. The amount of information you can convince prospects and leads to submit depends on how valuable your ebook is.

- Webinar gated landing pages are a valuable tool for qualifying leads at every stage of the funnel. If the information you're offering is relevant and it's delivered by an authoritative speaker, you can ask for several fields' worth of information to inform your marketing and sales teams.

- Demo gated landing pages are best used at the bottom of the funnel, because they offer a look at your product or service. These are people who have, through their own research and your top- and mid-funnel nurturing, determined that you're a finalist on their shortlist of solutions to their problem. Like selling to leads is about nurturing, nurturing is about qualifying. To nurture, you have to know your leads, and the best way to get to know them is with targeted, persuasive gated landing pages at every stage of the funnel.

Don't: inundate your sales team with leads

Generally, the belief is that the more leads marketing passes to the sales team, the better. But that's not always the case. It's very easy for the sales team (especially if it's a small one) to drown in leads, even if they're qualified. The more leads to contact, the more resources it takes to follow up. At Autocab we developed a points-based system in which visitors get "points" for each piece of content they consume – i.e. a web page is 1 point, an ebook is 20 points, and accessing the pricing page is 15. Only when a lead has accrued 60 points will the sales team be notified to make contact. Of course, should a lead request a demo at any point, this will go straight through to the sales team (along with a record of their content consumption thus far).

Consider qualifying your sales leads even further. Dig into data. Create more barriers between your prospect and your product.

While it may sound counterintuitive, when done right it will deliver fewer but more sales-ready leads that your team can keep up with. Done wrong, it could lead you to our next "don't"…

Don't: make lead qualifiers too narrow

Sure, qualifiers help your sales team find the most valuable leads quickly, but there's a balance. Sales leads qualified too broadly will waste your team's resources. If you're using company size and location as your only criteria, this may be you.

On the other hand, if your reps are waiting for sales leads all day, it's a good sign you've set the bar a little too high. If you're looking for 20, 30, 40 different criteria to qualify your leads for sale, you may be ignoring valuable, purchase-possible people.

Meet with your sales team regularly to check the quality of the leads coming through – it's not about quantity; it's about the quality.

...cont'd

Don't: set qualifiers and forget them

Qualifying leads isn't a set-it-and-forget-it kind of activity. Products, channels, and people all change. What was once working to deliver your best customer may no longer be.

You may find that with your new offering or feature you can expand into an entirely new market. Or, you may discover an even better channel on which to reach your target customer. Consider re-evaluating your standards once a quarter, and any time a big adjustment to your product is rolled out.

Even if leads drop out of the sales pipeline, add them to your "nurture" list – keep communicating to stay front-of-mind. One day they'll be ready to make a purchase.

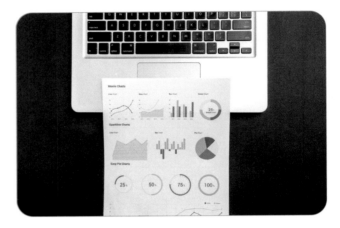

Don't: give up too quickly

According to research, if at first you don't qualify your lead, try, try again.

By making six calls, you have a 90% chance of qualifying your lead. Unfortunately, fewer than 5% of reps make that many calls. Most give up after one, and a staggering 30+% of leads are never even contacted.

You can increase your contact rate by up to 70% just by making a few more call attempts. So, why wouldn't you?

8 Building landing pages that convert

With a structured approach to creating your landing pages, you'll be able to zero in on what potential customers are looking for and offer exactly what they want, when they want it.

Simplicity is key

A website landing page should, in a single-page view, succinctly promote the product or service you're trying to sell. Whether it's a price promotion on a best-selling product, or an introductory 30-day free license for your software, a page visitor needs to understand exactly what's on offer, and understand the call to action (see page 133): complete a webform, click on a Buy button, or request a demo.

Let's break down this example from Shopify:

Call to action front and center – email address harvesting

No risk – try before you buy

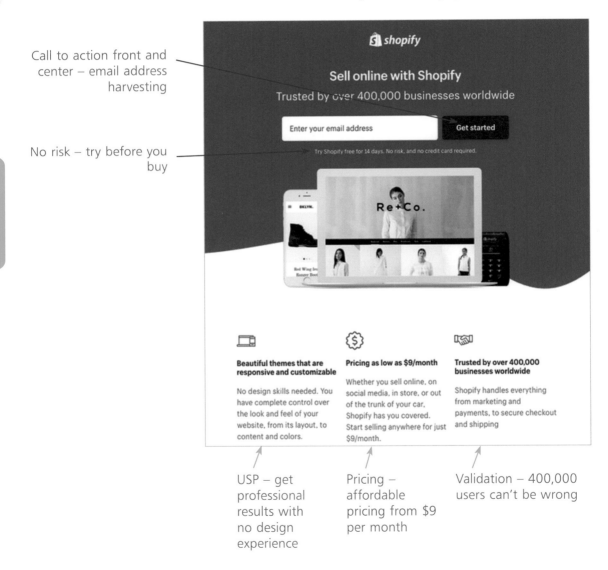

USP – get professional results with no design experience

Pricing – affordable pricing from $9 per month

Validation – 400,000 users can't be wrong

Cutting through the noise

Every Tom, Dick and Harry is trying to promote, sell, force their views, convert, inspire, turn on, and sometimes steal from hapless users of the World Wide Web. To decide that you want no part in the madness is terribly honorable but not terribly smart. You may have created a website that is content-rich, visually appealing and offers users deep analysis of each and every product feature you offer – but just because you provide it doesn't mean people are prepared to invest the time in finding it and consuming it. That's where product- or promotion-specific landing pages really help.

No business is operating in a vacuum, and that means there are competitors also fighting for your customers' attention. Not everyone will know your website address, or be following you already on social. In Chapter 4 (SEM & SEO) we learned how to create ads to drive traffic to your website – it is your landing page that will determine whether that user converts and becomes a customer. What is important is to ensure that however you decide to drive traffic to your site, when those visitors arrive they find a well-organized, visually pleasing place of interest, not a generic web page from your site with little or no reference to the ad or link that got them there.

Web users, by and large, are promiscuous – they will stay on a page for only so long as it continues to please them. When they've had their fill (or what they perceive to be all you have to offer) they move on to the next site. It is in those short few minutes, or seconds, depending on your performance, that you have the opportunity to hook them.

Hot tip

Click on some Google ads to see other companies' landing pages.

127

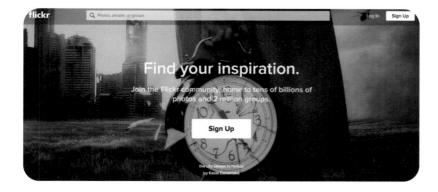

Crafting a message

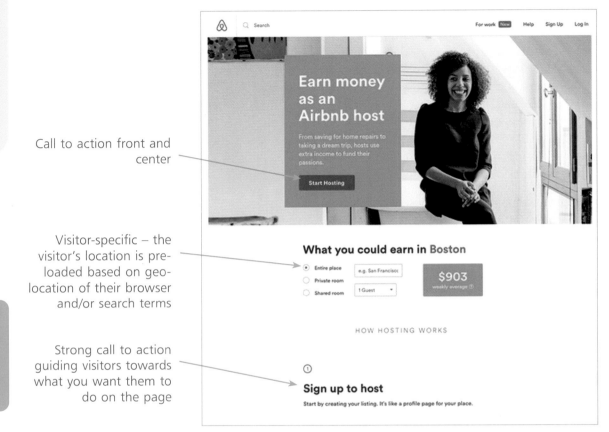

Call to action front and center

Visitor-specific – the visitor's location is preloaded based on geolocation of their browser and/or search terms

Strong call to action guiding visitors towards what you want them to do on the page

In the above example from Airbnb, we see how the company appeals to potential hosts by enticing homeowners to list their property on the platform by providing a simple location-specific calculator – which will show how much money they could make per night renting out their place: simple, effective and personalized.

Why simple landing pages work

The best landing pages are those that do not confuse. They are clear in their message about what they are promoting, whether that be a service provider, (e.g. financial services), a specific product (e.g. a new drink), or a concept (e.g. druid naming ceremonies). The landing page, no matter how many other products or services you provide, is geared towards this one purpose.

You can still show depth and breadth within the rest of the website, but this should not all be crammed onto the landing page. Get your user hooked, encourage them to interact with the call to action, and only then offer to lead them to the riches that are contained within the rest of your website.

In this example from Nauto, this is an email-harvesting landing page that offers the visitor value (a free ebook) in return for their personal details:

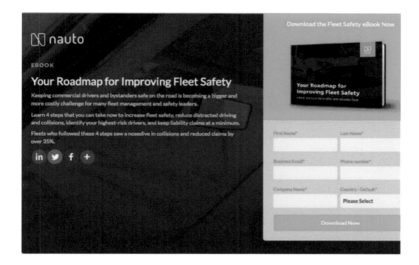

What won't work

The worst landing pages are those that try to alert the user to absolutely everything you have to offer – or that simply link through to your standard homepage. The site's owner feels that they are showcasing their entire offering; the visitor gets frightened, somewhat confused, and leaves. More commonly, a website will be full of claims reinforcing quality, excellence, excitement and professionalism – yet the actual site is slow, and badly designed and maintained. From this, the user will be quick to judge – the only thing being promoted is your desperation, not the desired effect.

It can take a little time getting used to working with the two interfaces.

Interactive landing pages

Moving on from the traditional forms and calls to action, check out this example from Landbot, which is itself a service that creates chatbot-based landing pages.

The firm is putting their own product front and center by incorporating a chat function within the landing page. When you land on this page, you're greeted by the bot (it's important to note that in the web version of this page, the GIF is animated and therefore very eye-catching). And by asking questions in a conversation, the bot is able to extract a lot more information than presenting visitors with a long form.

Whilst you are probably not a chatbot software provider, what's stopping you including a live chat function on your own landing pages? Enjoy instant engagement with your visitors with your own friendly bot, and convert visitors by being "available" to answer questions.

9 Optimizing your website

Not all websites are born equal – learn how to make your web pages work harder, be seen, be visited, and drive sales for your team and your business.

Benchmarking your website

When setting digital marketing goals and objectives, it is likely that a good percentage of businesses would have ticked "drive traffic to my website" as one of their top goals. The question is, once you have a solid digital marketing strategy and you are successfully driving traffic to your website, you need to ask yourself, "What are people seeing when they land on my site?".

You could have the most expensive website in the world that looks amazing from a design or technical point of view, but you're still not achieving those all-important conversions that a small business owner needs. However, the key features that your website needs to make it work from a marketing perspective are shown on the following pages of this chapter.

Have a look at your own website and see what your score is out of 10 on the checklist at the end of the chapter.

Calls to action

A call to action seems like quite a vague goal but, in simple terms, it means that you need to get your visitors to "do something" as soon as they land on the site, and they will need help deciding what to do. To convert a visitor to a consumer, you need them to do something to progress on the buyers' journey, such as **download**, **follow**, **click**, **join**, **subscribe**, **call**, **contact free helpline**, etc. These are the actions that make a real difference to those all-important conversions.

Here is a homepage that has some great calls to action:

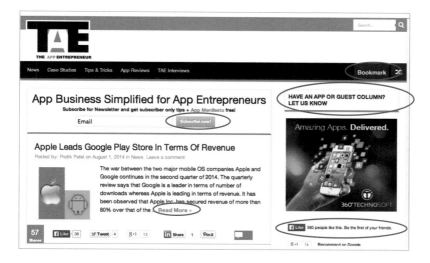

These are subtle, but effective. These actions help the visitor progress on their journey.

Keep it simple!

As a lead generation tool, it is imperative that you keep your calls to action as simple as possible. This is true on all platforms such as email marketing, press releases, blog posts, social media updates, etc. It is the easiest way to manipulate people's behavior in the way you want. Call-to-action (CTA) buttons have varied purposes, and thus a lot of thought and consideration needs to go into deciding what the call-to-action button aims to achieve.

Be careful and do not overload your homepage with too many calls to action. Make them subtle, with a focus on one or two main calls to action only.

Use customer-focused words within the content of your site.

The "We to You" ratio

As natural sales people, we feel that we want to tell the whole world about how good we are, how wonderful our products are, and the fabulous customer service that we offer. But visitors to your website only care about how you can help them meet their requirements. For this exercise, change hats and step into the shoes of a potential new customer that is visiting your website, whilst thinking about the following well-known saying:

> " *To sell John Brown,*
> *What John Brown buys,*
> *You must see the world*
> *Through John Brown's eyes.* "
>
> Unknown

So, now it is your turn to have a look at your own website and be honest. It's time to ask yourself the following questions:

Is it very obvious what your business does?

Is the site easy to navigate?

Does my site pass the "We to You" test?

What is the "We to You" test?

1 Look at the opening paragraph on your website and count how many company- or brand-focused words there are – words such as "we", "our", "us", and your own business name.

2 Next, count the number of customer-focused words such as "you" and "your".

3 Take the number of customer-focused words, divide it by the total number of words you counted up, then multiply the answer by 100 to get the percentage.

Ideally, the ratio should be at least balanced, or leaning in the direction of the customer. If you have an unhealthy ratio, then be aware that in the eyes of your visitor, the business invariably comes across as bragging to its readers, instead of talking to them. If your site is a bit "we we we", then I strongly suggest having a look at the content.

This is not an exact science, and I'm certainly not saying that "we" is a bad word, but when you use it, it's far better if you are talking about yourself in the context of that all-important "you": your customer.

> **So, how did you score on the "We to You" ratio? If you were more focused on your customer, then award yourself a point in this section.**

Fresh & unique content

This is discussed in more detail in Chapter 3 – Blogging. However, before you dismiss adding a blog or news to your website, then let's explain, in very basic terms, how Google has changed how it ranks a website. If "driving traffic to your website" was top of your goals list, then this section will be relevant to you and your business.

So, how does Google work?

100% S.E.O /Keywords/Meta tags/Link Baiting.

Beware

SEO tactics are not the only ingredient that Google looks for nowadays.

Back in the olden days (pre-2010), the main way of reaching page 1 of Google's search results pages (SERPs) was to manipulate your website (using SEO – search engine optimization – techniques). This meant that you would spend a lot of time, money and effort adding keywords, metatags, meta descriptions, inbound and outbound links, and registering your website with a glut of online directories such as DMOZ. In June 2010, Google decided to change the rules and announced to the world that no longer can you manipulate the system by simply optimizing your website.

With the introduction of a project known as Google Caffeine, a line was drawn in the sand against black-hat techniques looking to "trick" Google, and there were now three key elements involved if you wanted to be successful within Google Search. Although Caffeine has since been updated numerous times, (including the Maverick, Medic, and Maccabees updates), the fundamentals are still the same.

Optimize your website

It is still important to make sure that your website is keyword-rich and that your designers have optimized your site before submitting it to search engines. However, nowadays it is not the "be all and end all" of everything. There are two other elements to making sure that you have a chance in ranking on Google.

Create a buzz

Google (and other search engines) is no longer just looking at your website in order to give it a rating in the algorithm. Its spiders or robots are looking all over the internet to see if you are a good business worthy of being sent up the rankings. Google is everywhere. It is looking in open forums, on social networking platforms, blogging platforms, online newspapers, etc. If your business is being spoken about, or your content is being shared, then you will see a rise in the search engine listings. It is your responsibility to make your business and your content as popular as possible.

Fresh content

The critical factor for Google is new, fresh, unique content. This is what convinces Google your website is still current, important and influential. I'll explain:

Google will send its spiders or robots to have a look at your website. They will then collect all that good, juicy information and keywords and send it back to Google so that it can be indexed. A few weeks later, Google will resend those spiders back to your website, but this time they will only be looking for any new information on your site. That new information is then sent back to Google for ranking. But what happens if there is no new information on your website? Well, Google thinks to itself: "This company hasn't updated its site, so I will send my spiders back in four weeks' time to check." When the spiders come back in four weeks' time, and there is still no new information on the site, Google will say: "No new information; I will send my spiders back in three months' time", and so the cycle continues.

Having a social media presence is an important ingredient to your search engine optimization (SEO) within Google.

Adding a blog to your website is an easy way to regularly create fresh content.

137

...cont'd

Don't forget

The most influential ingredient to search engine optimization (SEO) is new, unique content on your website, so consider blogging.

If Google ranking is important to you, (which it should be!) then you need those little spiders to come back to your website as often as possible, so please feed them as much new, relevant information as you can.

As mentioned previously, Google likes new content on your website, but it gives more weight (or favoritism) to certain types of content. These are split into branded and unbranded content.

Branded content

Branded content simply means any pages on your website that are talking about your company. Good examples are the "About us", "Meet the team", and "Features and benefits of your products or services" sections, the "Contact us" page, or even a testimonial page. These pages are known as "branded content" and it is important to change and update these pages as regularly as possible, but it does not have as much impact on the Google algorithm as "unbranded content".

Unbranded content

Unbranded content is content that has the visitor in mind rather than your business. Google favors content that your visitors find interesting and helpful. Examples of good "unbranded content" are:

- Frequently asked questions (FAQs) page.
- Toolkit.
- Blogs/news or articles that are about your industry and relevant to your audience (not blogs about your new employee, or how you have raised lots of money in a charity event that you did at the weekend).

If you do have a blog or a news feature on your website then we recommend adding an article as an absolute minimum at least once every two weeks (800-1,500 words). The more content you create, the better your chances are of being indexed.

> **Do you regularly update the content on your website to keep the Google spiders happy? If "yes", then give yourself a point.**

Make sure that the content you are posting is relevant to your industry, sector, product or business. If you constantly provide irrelevant content, it won't impact your ranking.

Harvesting emails

As any good marketer will tell you, email is probably the most powerful tool to talk directly to your audience. There were many blogs floating around the internet a few years ago saying that email will soon be dead, and people will just communicate on social networking platforms. There will probably always be a place for email, as well as the telephone, and even printed matter. Capturing those all-important email addresses from your website visitors is a no-brainer, but so many people go about it in the wrong way.

The words "subscribe to our newsletter" can be considered as words of doom. People are so worried about spam and privacy nowadays that they become reluctant to enter their email address into those types of forms.

Visitors to your site will provide their email address to you if they feel that they are getting something value-added in return. A free ebook, (see more about this in Chapter 7 – Marketing automation) or a special offer, a discount coupon, techniques on a specific subject, the first chapter of a book, registering for job alerts, legal updates, property searches… the list is endless. The important part is what you do with that email address once you have received it.

> **General Data Protection Regulation (GDPR): If you wish to harvest the email addresses of visitors based in Europe, then those visitors MUST opt in to receive emails from you (see Don't forget tip on page 41).**

Beware

Avoid using the terminology "subscribe to our newsletter".

Social sharing tools

Please do not confuse these with "social media links". Social sharing tools (otherwise known as social proof buttons), are a fantastic way for your content to be shared by your audience.

In this picture (from **Sharethis.com**) they clearly display the power of a good social sharing tool. You can see that 7.6k people have clicked on one of the social share buttons and shared this article on their social media platforms, therefore driving more traffic back to their website.

Remember that Google loves it when people share your content, so make it easy for your visitors to do this.

This is a powerful tool and one not to be ignored. The key items that you should be adding a social sharing tool to are:

- Your blogs or news articles.
- Your frequently asked questions (FAQs) page.
- Your special offers or free downloads.
- Your jobs (if you're a recruiter), or properties if you're an estate agent/realtor.
- Your toolkit page.

If you would like to add social sharing buttons to your website, try **www.sharethis.com**. This is a floating toolbar (as seen in the example above), and will stay with your visitor as they read your article. It is much more effective than having a sharing tool at the top of your article, or at the bottom.

If you only have social sharing tools for Facebook and Twitter but your main target market is more business-to-business (B2B), then consider adding LinkedIn (see Chapter 13).

> **Do you have social sharing tools on your website? If you can answer "yes", then congratulations – you have another tick in the box!**

Social media links

Do you have social media icons on the homepage of your website?

It is also worth noting that usually there is no reason for a company to be present on ALL social networking platforms. It is only advisable to have a presence on the social networking sites where your target market is present.

Here is a list of social networking sites that are usually present on websites as clickable icons:

- Twitter
- Facebook
- LinkedIn
- YouTube
- Pinterest
- Instagram

Key social networking sites are discussed in more detail later in the book. However, if your target market is not active on a particular platform, then there is no point in wasting time, money and effort in trying to make it work. Spend that valuable time and money on platforms that work for you.

If you have social media icons with links on your website, then you cannot quite tick the box yet! Check to see that all the links go to the right places.

For example:

Introducing Autocab

...cont'd

When you click on the Facebook icon, you will be redirected to the company Facebook page; likewise with Twitter and the YouTube account.

Double-check that your icons are not social sharing tools as this often confuses your audience. Social sharing tools should not be visible in the header, as it is on this example below.

Check that the link your LinkedIn icon goes to is your **company** page, and not your **personal** profile.

These are social sharing tools, NOT links to your social networking sites

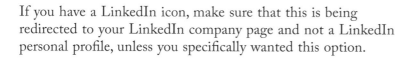

If you have a LinkedIn icon, make sure that this is being redirected to your LinkedIn company page and not a LinkedIn personal profile, unless you specifically wanted this option.

> **Do you have your social media links on the homepage of your website and, if so, do they redirect to all the right places? If yes, then give yourself a point.**

143

Is your site mobile friendly?

It's no secret that the mobile web is growing, and growing fast. It seems impossible to go out in public without seeing someone with a smartphone in their hand. What many may not realize is just how powerful the mobile web is actually becoming. With more and more people accessing the internet from their mobile devices, websites that aren't optimized for mobile may become lost in the fold.

Did you know that in 2019 the percentage of all global web pages served to mobile phones was 52.6%, making it more likely that your visitors are now accessing your website via phone rather than desktop or laptop? So, how do you know if your site is mobile friendly, apart from the obvious and looking at the site on your own smartphone or tablet?

Visit **https://ready.mobi/** and test your website for free. This software displays your website on a variety of smartphones and tablets so you can see what your visitors will be viewing.

Sometimes it is not necessary to have a fully responsive website, but there are some key elements that you do need to consider:

- Can the text be easily read without scrolling, pinching or zooming?
- Can customers call you with a single press of a button?
- Are page links large enough to click with your thumb?
- If you are a retailer, is your store locator visible on the Home screen?
- Does your website look professional and inviting to use?

Did your website pass the mobile-friendly test? If so, then please allocate yourself a point in the checklist at the end of this chapter.

Including a phone number

It is a well-known fact that the more visitors have to click within your site to find the information that they need, the more it dilutes that all-important conversion. You have probably visited websites in the past, and even on the "Contact us" page there is no phone number, or sometimes not even an email address; there may only be a box to complete with details of your message. As a consumer, this is highly frustrating, when all you want is to talk to someone.

It is possibly one of the simplest additions you can make to your website, and yet so few businesses think it's worthwhile… adding your phone number.

Hot tip

Having a telephone number visible in the header of your website is paramount for most small business owners. However, if you do include this in the header of your website, the phones should be managed during normal working hours as it's even more frustrating for customers if the phone isn't answered or they have to wait in a queue for a long time. If providing telephone support isn't viable, then it's best to put your contact number on the "Contact us" page rather than your homepage.

As you can see in this example (**www.jackrosen.com**), Jack offers customized kitchens and has placed his company phone number at the top of every page on his website. This is a "complex sale", which won't ever be closed by a customer simply adding a kitchen to their basket and paying with a card online. Rather, Jack's website is a sales tool, to whet the appetite and show a selection of previous custom kitchens and the company's design and build quality. Jack needs potential customers to like what they see and then reach out and make contact. Sure, an online webform is useful for capturing their data, and someone can call them back. The offer of an email address is useful too, and some customers will choose to write to Jack and request more information. But without doubt, a large number of potential customers are going to want to phone up and ask their questions. If the company phone number isn't easily visible, then there's a chance Jack might not get that call… or that customer.

...cont'd

Again, in this example Rick has elected to add his phone number to the top navigation of his website. Anyone with questions or concerns can phone and ask, and get the answers they seek quickly and effectively.

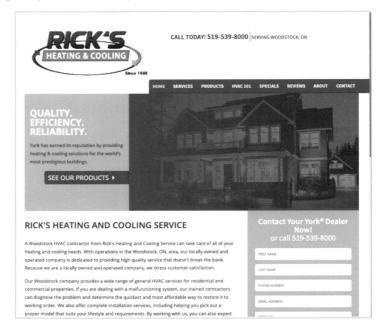

There are a number of arguments why you shouldn't make your phone number clearly visible – for example, a high-volume e-commerce store with limited staff worried that they will be inundated with calls. But if you have a B2B, or a very specialist B2C, offering anything that would class as a "complex sale", then I would strongly suggest you include a phone number on your website and celebrate, rather than hide, the fact that you are happy to take calls from customers and prospects.

> **Does your website have a visible telephone number on the homepage of your website? If "yes", then please allocate yourself a point in the checklist at the end of this chapter.**

Testimonials & reviews

Nothing can make or break your company quicker than people talking. The fact is, we are human beings and people listen to what others say. It is probably more important than ever to make those words count.

Before you make the decision to skip this section because you are of the mindset "I do not want to add my clients onto my website for my competitors to find out who my clients are", then please take five minutes to read this section of the book.

We all know how fast bad news can travel. If someone is unhappy with your product or service, then they are more likely to talk about it. (See the Reputation management section on pages 27-28.)

If your business has 20 testimonials or positive reviews on its website, then this will far outweigh the one negative comment that people may say online about your business.

If your competitors are any good, then they will already know who your clients are. If a competitor views a testimonial on my website, I feel that the message I am sending out to those competitors is "I have this awesome relationship with this client, so beware competitors!".

Avoid "wet lettuce" testimonials. Here are examples of wet lettuce testimonials:

"Very Positive! Staff are always helpful and obliging. Also you found me the exact job that I wanted in the location that I wanted."
Community Safety Officer

"In the 15 months I contracted I was placed five times and eventually into a permanent position. Excellent support. Always paid on time, never needed to doubt that I would be placed. Was always certain of a placement and therefore an income."
IT Support & Training Officer

...cont'd

The website this is from had over 20 testimonials. However, there may be some doubt about the credibility of the content. Who is IT Support & Training Officer? Your website visitors will also be doubting your credibility if you have vague testimonials like this. Therefore, why would you highlight this on your website?

The video testimonial is a powerful weapon in the content marketer's arsenal.

The video testimonial

Having a customer give a video testimonial is probably the most powerful of all testimonials, as you can see the whites of their eyes and see how genuine they are. Adding a video testimonial on YouTube and then linking to this from your own website is also an additional way of increasing your search engine optimization (SEO). Remember, Google owns YouTube. There's much more on using video more effectively on pages 36-37.

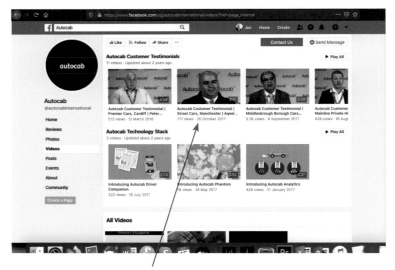

The more customer video testimonials you can feature, the better

Trustpilot

Reputations are hard to forge and easy to lose. Whatever you are planning to sell online, you need to gain new customers' trust before they will be willing to buy from you.

As a new business with a limited customer base, the best way to instill trust is to turn your customers into advocates by letting them review your products and service. E-commerce platforms such as Shopify, BigCommerce and Magento offer customer review plugins and extensions that are simple to deploy.

Probably the best-known third-party review service is Trustpilot. Hundreds of thousands of websites have integrated Trustpilot to allow their customers to review them in a bid to drive growth. Here's why:

Check out **www. audioboom.com** to record your audio testimonials and add them to your website. Easily accessible via an app on Android or iOS phones.

1 Increase organic search traffic – a customer is more likely to click through to a website with a high star rating than one without.

2 Improve the click-through rate (CTR) from paid ads – by embedding your star rating in your adverts, customers will be drawn to your ad over those of your competitors.

3 Boost conversions and sales – other customers have clearly taken the plunge and ordered from you. Their positive reaction will inspire others to do the same.

...cont'd

Case studies

Having a full case study, or completed portfolio, is also very powerful on your website. The more detail, the better.

Adding a testimonial/review or case study to your website helps to give your potential clients confidence that you are worth doing business with. Feeling comfortable with you, your product and your professionalism is often the main reason why people will, or will not, do business with you.

Do you have credible testimonials or reviews on your website? If "yes", then give yourself a point in the checklist at the end of this chapter.

Do you offer a guarantee?

Today's new generation of bloggers and entrepreneurs have discovered that having a guarantee, an age-old offline technique, can be one of the most powerful routes to more sales.

They know that online buyers are plagued by fears and doubts. And there's nothing that will kill a sale faster than doubt.

"But putting a guarantee on my website can be a high risk", I hear you think aloud. This is so not true and is a complete misconception.

So, what makes a good guarantee? Here are some ideas for you:

Look at your competitors
What are they guaranteeing to their customers?

Look at your strengths
What area of your business do you excel in? Do you do fast installations? Do you respond quickly to a customer? Do you have the widest selection in town? Do you save money for your customers?

Guarantee results
This could be delivery times or good things that happen when customers use your products: Better relationships? More money? Reduced stress? Write down the answer in specific detail, and then guarantee that outcome. (Just make sure you can fulfill your promise.)

Choose a payback
Remember, only a small volume of customers will ever take you up on a payback. You want to create an attractive payback in case customers are unsatisfied. Ideally, it won't cost you much but will have a high perceived value. A hassle-free, money-back guarantee is a good place to start. But try to dress it up a bit. Remember, a better-than-risk-free guarantee is the best guarantee of all. Yours should exceed customer expectations and be memorable.

Having numerous guarantees on your site to instill confidence in the various products and services that you provide will enhance the possibility of those all-important sales conversions.

> **Do you have a guarantee on your website? If so, then please award yourself a point in the checklist at the end of this chapter.**

Don't forget

Remember, your potential buyers feel a certain level of risk whenever you offer something to them. A guarantee is your best tool for lowering or eliminating that risk.

Check out the legal requirements for your own country. For instance:

UK: https://www. gov.uk/running-a-limited-company/ signs-stationery-and-promotional-material

US: http://legalzoom.com

Canada: https://www. canadabusiness.ca/eng/ page/2764/

Australia: https:// www.business.gov.au/ Marketing/Marketing-and-advertising/Business-marketing

Beware

If you are requesting visitors to surrender their personal details, then make sure you have a privacy policy on your website.

Don't forget

If your website is collecting cookies, it is a legal requirement in the UK to have a pop-up cookie policy.

Important & legal information

If your business is a registered limited company in the UK, for instance, then it is a legal requirement to display your company details. You are required to add the following on your website: your company's registered name; place of registration; company registration number; and registered office address.

This could be added as a footnote to your homepage, an addition on the "Contact us" or "About us" page, or within your terms of business.

If your website collects user data (i.e. you may have a "Contact us" form, or an opt-in form where people need to leave their email address), you must display a privacy policy informing the user what the business does with the data and that it conforms to the Data Protection Act.

If you are using Google Analytics (see Chapter 15), or other visitor-analysis packages, or any type of CMS (content management system), the law in the UK requires you to retrieve consent from your visitors that it is OK for you to monitor and record their activity on your site, and a whole bunch of other information. Just having a small note about how you use cookies in your terms of business is not acceptable. You need a cookie policy pop-up that is visible immediately to the visitor as soon as they land on your website. This website is very helpful: **https://www.seqlegal.com/**

Check online before implementing any new procedures on your site, as these rules often change.

Conclusion

The four steps to website marketing success:

 Build your platform

Hopefully you scored high in the steps described in this chapter, which means that you have achieved stage one for building your website.

 Grow your network

If you have implemented a data-capture process, added numerous pages that are "unbranded content", and consistently drip fed your audience with good blogs, articles, news or events, then you have achieved stage two – grow your network.

3 **Define a listening, engagement and content strategy**

Have you activated comments in your news? Have you put together a marketing plan for your content on your site? Have you set up a listening strategy, and registered with **mention.com**? If so, then you have achieved stage three – define a strategy.

4 **Measure the results**

Have you got Google Analytics on your site? Have you set your Google Analytics goals? Are you looking at your statistics? Do you know where your traffic is coming from? What is your bounce rate? How many unique visitors do you have to your site each week? Is this increasing? Do you know where you are ranked in Google? If you have the answers to all these questions, and you are regularly monitoring and tweaking your site to improve its performance, then you have accomplished stage four and you are on your way to website marketing success.

See Chapter 15 for more on Google Analytics.

Checklist

How did you score on the 10-point checklist for your website?

 Do you have "calls to action" on your homepage? ☐

 Is your "We to You" ratio healthy? ☐

3 Are you adding new content to your website on a regular basis? ☐

4 Do you have a data-capture process? ☐

5 Are there social sharing tools on your site? ☐

6 Do you have social media links on the homepage of your website and do they go to the right place? ☐

7 Is your site mobile friendly? ☐

8 Do you have a visible contact number in the header? ☐

9 Do you have credible testimonials, case studies or reviews on your website? ☐

10 Do you offer a guarantee? ☐

10 Instagram

An introduction to Insta

Without doubt there's a lot of hype surrounding Instagram (commonly referred to as Insta), and how it can impact your business and drive new and repeat custom. But should you actually believe it?

The answer is a resounding "yes"! With, at the time of writing, just over one billion registered active users and a staggering 500 million using the platform every single day, it's no longer a choice to get your brand onto Instagram – it's a business necessity!

But if you're not one of those existing users, the most common question is "How can I use this platform to promote my business?".

As with each of the chapters in this book, follow the steps; understand what you're doing and why to give yourself the very best chance of driving brand success on this important social network. You're about to learn:

- All the basics, from setting up a business account to setting ambitious yet achievable goals.
- How to take amazing photos and ensure your account is brimming with great visual content that's perfect for the platform.
- The most effective ways to analyze your content and measure your results to prove your work makes a difference.

Plus, you'll learn everything you need to know about different post formats, how to leverage Instagram stories, and more.

Don't forget

Just because you don't use an app personally doesn't mean that you should discount it from your digital marketing arsenal.

Getting started

The very first thing to do in order to start marketing on Instagram is to set up a business account. I can't stress enough that you should take some time to use Instagram yourself before using it too heavily for your business (if you're not someone who already uses it personally).

Optimizing your Instagram business profile

Next, make sure your profile is completely optimized. This means:

- **Writing a compelling bio**. You have 150 characters to summarize what your business is about.
- **Use a recognizable profile image**. Your logo is typically a sound choice.
- **Choose a good profile link**. On Instagram, links are only allowed on profiles (and not on posts). Two options are your brand's website homepage or a link to a new page or piece of content you're promoting.

Check out the Insta accounts of your competitors and brands you admire to begin to formulate your own idea of how you want to present your brand.

Who to follow?

When you're first starting out, you'll need to choose accounts to follow. Here are some types of accounts to think about starting with:

- **Your partner brands**. Companies you work with are a great place to start.
- **Influencers in your niche**. These are people and brands that your audience follows. Start by searching a few keywords for accounts related to your brand or product.
- **Brands you're inspired by**. This will help you get ideas for your own posts and campaigns.
- **Your competitors**. It's essential to keep tabs on what they're up to.

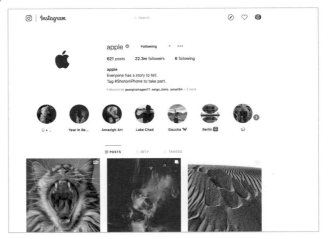

While doing so, note what type of content works for them, and find out what your competitors are doing. Ask yourself these questions:

- What draws you to their Instagram posts?
- How often are they posting?
- What do you dislike about their posts?
- What type of information do they include in their profile?
- Is there a consistent theme?

Keep what you learn in mind for later.

Your Instagram goals

Once you have some research and inspiration stored away, it's time to think about your business. What are your goals as a company? Here are some Instagram goals you might want to focus on:

- Increasing your follower count.
- Growing your brand awareness.
- Greater engagement.

Whatever your goal might be, make sure it's clear and concise so that you can always refer to it throughout your Instagram process. It's essential (for Instagram and, in fact, any goal setting) that your goals are specific, measurable, attainable, relevant, and time-based – known as SMART goals. For example, a great goal would be:

"We want to increase our following by 15% over the course of the next month."

This goal is specific in which metric to track, states the desired outcome, and has a clear deadline for that outcome.

Hot tip

Add your Instagram account to your email signature – with more people accessing their mail via phone, a link to an Insta account is far more appealing than a website.

159

Aligning Instagram metrics with business objectives

Growing an Instagram following and getting tons of engagement on your posts is great.

But if your goals aren't connected to actual business outcomes, then they don't matter much.

So, when you're setting goals, know how you're aiming to improve your brand each time you post. To do this, select metrics to track that help drive certain business objectives.

How to measure Instagram

It can't be stressed enough how important this one is.

Whether you're starting out or revamping your current Instagram profile, it's time to start recording your data!

Remember that one aspect of SMART goals: measurable? If you can't track your efforts, you'll never be able to see if your strategy is working.

Use Google Sheets or Excel to track the analytics behind your posts. Make sure to record these five elements of every Instagram post from here on out:

1 Date.

2 Total followers.

3 Type of post (e.g. culture, product, inspiration, etc.).

4 Time.

5 Engagement after x amount of time.

Record your data from every Instagram post				
Date	Followers	Type of Post	Time	Impressions/ Engagement
04-Oct	2046	product	11.23am	1035 / 212
05-Oct	2081	culture	11.40am	890 / 190
06-Oct	3015	inspiration	12.05pm	721 / 187
07-Oct	3376	product	12.22pm	1312 / 256

Once you have this data from all of your posts, you'll be able to make smart, strategic decisions every time you post. Find what works, take out what doesn't, and watch it grow your Instagram account.

Then, track your performance for each post over time.

Instagram content strategy

Now, before you go posting just anything on Instagram, understand why you're creating that content in the first place. Everything you post should have a purpose, support your goals, and strengthen your brand. Outlining a simple content strategy can help achieve these aims.

Start with your story

The most important step in defining your strategy is to brainstorm how you can connect the story of your product to your audience. What was the original idea that made your business idea come to life? Take that and run with it.

For example, Lululemon was founded on the idea that working out together could also cultivate community.

Beware

Is there a purpose to every one of your posts? If not, don't post.

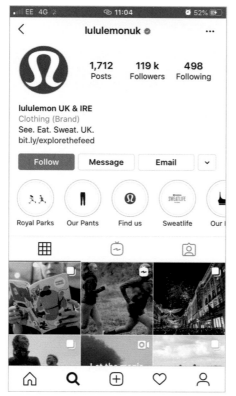

According to their website: "Our vision for our store was to create more than a place where people could get gear to sweat in, we wanted to create a community hub where people could learn and discuss the physical aspects of healthy living, mindfulness and living a life of possibility."

...cont'd

The idea was simple: health and community to live a fuller life. That is their story.

On their Instagram account, that same narrative continues to tells the story among all of their posts.

It's almost instantly evident what they're about, and it's consistent across their entire page.

Don't rush to fill your gallery with images – better to have a few great images that really sell your brand rather than a ton of mediocre images.

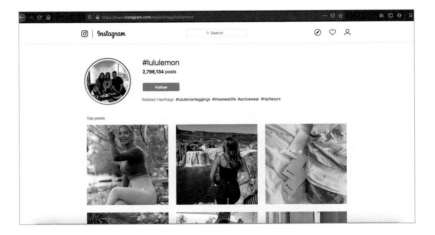

In order to find your own narrative, ask yourself these three questions:

1 What is the core idea behind your product?

2 What do people love about your product?

3 What would your audience miss about your business if you stopped tomorrow?

These three questions will help shape your story. Combine your narrative with your goal, and now you have a strategy.

Which post types work best?

Now that you have an awesome strategy in place, it's time to decide which types of posts you want to share with your audience. Every audience is different, so trying out different types of posts to see what works will be very beneficial for both audience building and increased engagement.

1. **Inspiration**: Inspirational posts are really great for motivating your audience. Who doesn't need a good morning pick-me-up? Inspirational posts often come in the form of quotes, so find some key people who believe in your narrative and/or goal, and use that as a starting point.

2. **Company culture**: Culture posts are ones that truly align with the heart-and-core values of your business. It could be for fun and play, or something you personally support. Culture posts are great for being transparent and honest with your audience. Show them who you really are! Let them share in your funny "behind the scenes" or "a day in the office" posts.

3. **Product posts**: While they may be the most obvious, product posts are one of the most essential Instagram types to use. After all, the ever-present goal is always to grow your business, right? Instagram is a great platform to show off how your products work, promote new stuff, and get people interested in what you have to offer.

4. **Event photos**: Attending a conference? Hosting an event? Snap some shots for Instagram.

5. **Interesting statistics**: Everyone loves a fact or figure that sounds almost impossible to believe but is totally accurate. Statistics that help businesses make decisions are great, too.

6. **Designed images**: Event flyers, ads, and other such items would fall under this category.

Hot tip

Consider giving your staff the "keys" to your Insta account – they can take turns taking photos and uploading posts. Improve your company culture and create an active account in one go!

163

Instagram done right

It'll be helpful to see some examples of what good Instagram posts look like. Here's a handful to check out:

Inspiration from Bluetick

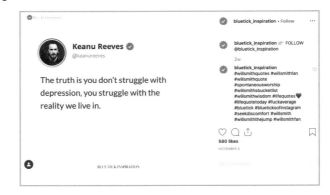

Product from Nike

Event video post from Red Bull

Interesting stats from ESPN

Designed image from ModCloth

Culture from Hootsuite

Don't be tempted to use images from another company's Insta feed unless you credit them.

Building your style

One of the unique qualities about Instagram, among all the other social platforms, is that it's primarily visual with its ongoing feed of imagery. This allows businesses to visually show off their product, rather than just tell; however, this also presents a challenge.

How can you make your business narrative be seen through a consistent, visually appealing brand? Here are some key factors that will ensure your Instagram feed looks great and tells your story well.

The bare essentials

While top-notch, expensive camera gear surely has its benefits, it's definitely not required to have a great visual presence on Instagram.

What you do need is a smartphone with a camera, and some good natural light. Whether you're taking photos of people experiencing the benefits of your product outside or you're taking photos of physical products indoors, these two are essential to get going.

Your smartphone is enough to get started – the latest phones have amazing built-in cameras.

Natural lighting

Quality lighting for your photos can take them to the next level! The best lighting source is found outside, but there are also ways to capture this gorgeous light indoors.

If you want to take your photo outside, the best time of day for lighting is called the golden hour – just after sunrise or before sunset when the skies turn golden and make everything seem magical. Depending on where you live, taking photos at those times of day may not be ideal, so if you need to take photos in the middle of the day here are some tips:

1. **Avoid direct, high-noon sun outside**. In the middle of the day, the sun is directly above, which can cast harsh shadows on your subject. Instead, we want an evenly-lit subject, so to avoid the bright sun, find some shade. In the shade, your image will have even light, making for a wonderful photo.

2. **Avoid dark, indoor spaces**. While it's common to have offices and buildings with tiled, white fluorescent lighting in the ceiling, this is not ideal for your images because it will make them appear yellow. Instead, try finding a room with a window so that you'll capture the great natural lighting while still being inside.

3. **Use a reflector**. If you can't go outside and you don't have any windows nearby, you can purchase a reflector for about $20/£15 to help you bounce the available light onto your subject.

Choosing a filter

Once you've taken your image with great lighting, and have saved your image, it's time to edit it!

The first thing you'll want to do is choose your filter. Filters are several different style and editing presets that are ready to use. There are an extremely high number of filter options out there today from a variety of apps, including Instagram's 21 default filter options, so be careful when you choose your filter.

Ask yourself this:

- Does this filter reflect the mood of my business narrative?
- Does this filter draw attention to itself or does it enhance my subject in the photo?
- Is this filter consistent with my other imagery?

Don't forget

Keep an eye out for new filters released by Instagram and third parties.

Once you've chosen a filter or two that works best for your business, make sure to stick with that filter.

While it's okay to experiment right away, too many different filters at once can disrupt the mood and emotion of your Instagram feed as a whole. When your audience goes to your account and sees nine images together, consistency needs to be evident in telling your story.

Downloading some popular Instagram tools

From start to finish, there are apps and tools out there to help you get the best photo possible. Here's a list of some of my favorite photo tools, from creation to hitting the Publish button:

1. **Snapseed**: Once you've taken your image, open it in Snapseed for several advanced editing tools and filters.

2. **Filterstorm Neue**: While only available for iPhone, the app has a diverse collection of customizable editing options.

3. **TouchRetouch**: Need to edit out something? This app is perfect for detailed retouching!

4. **ProCamera**: If you'd like more control of your iPhone camera, this app allows you the full functionality.

Explore the different options, and see what works best for you. Every workflow is unique, so choose an app that matches your photo process best.

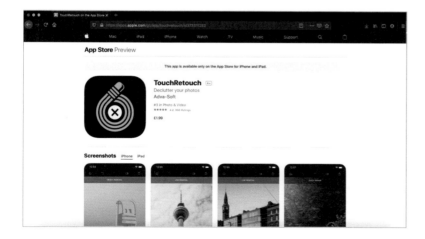

Growing your audience

First of all, congrats! You've thoroughly developed your Instagram strategy, created some awesome Instagram posts, recorded your data, and now it's time to optimize everything for the next level of audience engagement!

At this point, you know what works well, and you're ready to fine-tune everything to achieve your goals faster and better. There are six easy steps to optimizing your entire Instagram account, from the descriptions and imagery to tagging others and building a community.

Instagram is all about striking visuals. But having the perfect caption can help give your images better context and make them more engaging. Follow these guidelines every time you write post copy:

Using hashtags

Hashtags are really important to your Instagram posts because they allow others that may not have heard of your product before to find you. They let you reach a broader audience, and who doesn't want that?

An easy way to find which hashtags are currently trending is to use all-hashtag.com – this provides a nice, clear list with the highest rated hashtags and how many posts currently have that hashtag. It also lets you click on the hashtag to see examples of how others are using it.

How many hashtags should you use? That's a great question.

Instagram allows you to use up to 30 hashtags for each post, but it's best practice to use between 5-10. While the more hashtags, the better, it is always important to remember to avoid being spammy. You can find the perfect amount of hashtags to use by doing two things:

- Look at which other hashtags the influencers in your industry are using and how many.
- Test your own Instagram posts with a variety of hashtag amounts, and see what works best.

Tag industry influencers

In order to grow your community, look to the big influencers and see how you can involve them in your Instagram strategy.

Not only can you learn from them, but you can easily share their quotes, products, and other resources within your own posts that align with your business's narrative. For example, I am a big fan of marketing guru Seth Godin and his mantras so I've read a lot of his content.

When you share content from others, make sure your posts are still original. Take your own images, design your own quote graphics, and still create something that matches your own business, but remember to give them credit. Tag them in your posts so that they see it, their audience might see it, and then watch your audience grow.

...cont'd

Adding a location

Every Instagram post has the option to add a location to it.

This is yet another way Instagram users can search to find people to follow.

If your business is known especially in a specific region, this is even more valuable! You can either search for your location and find it using maps, or you can create your own custom location. Custom locations can be especially helpful for business events, as you can add a personal touch.

Using Instagram locations is a simple extra way to allow your potential audience to find you.

Optimize your link in your profile

Instagram has a very minimal profile space to personalize the information to your business and its goals, so businesses must take advantage of what they're given.

One of the best ways to do so is by updating and modifying your link for each Instagram post. While a best practice is to have your business or product website link there on a long-term basis, feel free to customize that link with posts that direct your audience to something more specific.

Do you have a feature launch coming up? Was your business just featured on a reputable news source? Use those opportunities to post about it on Instagram, and directly link to it in your profile.

This allows your audience to avoid mistyping anything, and gives instant access to precisely what you want them to see. Just remember to add "link in profile" to your Instagram post description, and then they'll know to hit the link in your profile.

Know how often to post

Frequency is a major factor when publishing to Instagram. On one hand, you don't want to post so often that it looks spammy and turns away your followers, but on the other you want enough posts to continually build up your Instagram community.

According to Buffer, the top brands post about 1.5 times per day. So, what does that mean for you? Let's test it:

For each week that you recorded, count how many Instagram posts you've published. Then, take your first day of the week's follower count and your last day of the week's follower count, and find the difference. Do this same process for every week that you've published content.

What do you notice? Are there some weeks that have a lot of posts but lower follower growth? Or did posting a lot triple your follower count?

Your business is unique, and so will your data be. Take the time to analyze and reflect, and you'll be amazed at the results.

Advertise with Instagram

Instagram ads get a 2.8-times-higher response rate than other forms of online advertising.

Once you know what type of Instagram post works, it's time to make it an ad and let it work for you! Instagram ads are integrated with Facebook ads and can be in the form of image, video, or carousel style, where multiple images are in a scroll for your audience to tap through.

Using what you already know, you can simply promote your posts to go just a bit further, making a big difference. Instagram advertising is great for businesses because it's yet another thing you can measure to reach your goals. Not only that; it adds a direct call to action in your ads that can lead your audience directly to your product.

Beware

If you're new to digital advertising, start with a very limited budget to test the water. Once you understand which campaigns work, and why, increase your limits.

Instagram best practices

That might seem to be a lot to remember, so let's go over the best practices. If you must take away one thing, or maybe three, these would be it.

Brand: focus on what's unique about you

- Every product has a story to tell that's unique and personal to the heart of the company.
- Which idea initially inspired the business?
- Which problem did it solve?

Find that story, and tell it to the world with Instagram... over and over again. Emphasize why it matters and how your business can help. Utilize your unique business narrative in the brand of your Instagram account from what you say to how you show it.

Craft: be thoughtful about what you share

Quality beats quantity. While you do want to build up your posting schedule over time, it's even more important that you spend time on each and every post, making it thoughtful, even if that means one Instagram post a week.

Take out your phone, find some natural light, use the rule of thirds and take a quality photo. Think about how your brand narrative connects with that image, and then craft your description. Your audience will immediately be able to distinguish your quality content over others' average content.

Community: engage, interact, and participate

Instagram was founded on the idea of community and bringing people together, so let's use it that way! If you want your brand and product to grow, make sure to interact with your followers, comment on others' posts, create Instagram stories, and follow other major industry influencers. Whenever you can, be personable and share behind the scenes. This will not only grow your close community, but spread your internal culture to your audience.

You might sell widgets that aren't particularly photogenic – but that doesn't stop you from using Instagram to showcase your staff, culture or where your widgets end up... with your customers!

11 Facebook

Facebook is the most visited social network in the world – your customers are on it... are you?

An introduction to Facebook

Facebook is a fantastic marketing tool for many businesses, but it is not for everyone. The first question you need to ask yourself is "Do I need to be active on Facebook?". If your target market is not on Facebook, if this is not a platform where they are talking, then don't waste your time, effort and money here.

What are the demographics for Facebook?

As you can see, although the biggest demographic on Facebook is 25-34 year-olds, there is now representation of all age groups across Facebook, meaning that whatever your target age group, you'll find them on Facebook.

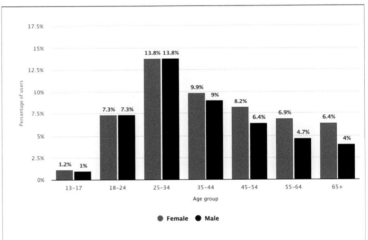

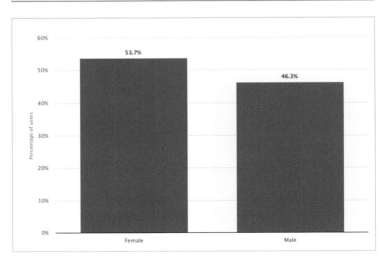

There is not much of a difference between a male and female split, which is nice to see.

Don't forget

Facebook pages may vary, so the graphics that are showcased in this book may not look exactly the same as your Facebook page. Facebook is forever rolling out new features, and deleting old ones, so your page may not represent all of the features named in this book.

Don't forget

66% of users check Facebook every single day.

176

> **Total Number of Mobile Active Users:**
>
> 2.26 billion (source)
>
> Last updated: 9/4/19
>
> **Total Number of Desktop Active Users:**
>
> 1.47 billion (source)
>
> Last updated: 9/4/19

Most striking is the rapid increase of Facebook users accessing the platform via mobile devices, which now outnumber those accessing it via a desktop computer. What does that mean for your business? Post frequent, short posts, and utilize images and video rather than just text to capitalize on this trend.

Which industries thrive on Facebook?

Let us showcase some exceptionally good Facebook pages that were featured on HubSpot's list of Best Facebook Business Page Examples Online Today.

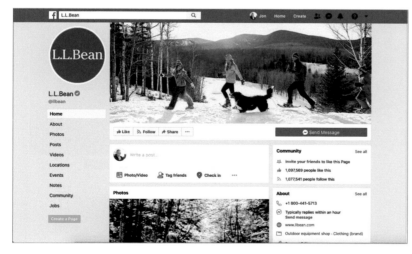

What HubSpot liked:

"This is an example of a Facebook page that focuses on the customer. The content they post is interesting and super relevant for their target audience: cool photos, videos, and tips for outdoor adventures. They also include tabs dedicated to their events, open job opportunities, and to each of their most recent grand openings."

...cont'd

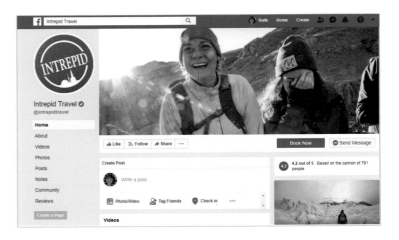

What HubSpot liked:

"Travel agency Intrepid Travel has put together a great Facebook page – complete with a special tab that shows trip and tour reviews, and one that lets users search and book trips without having to leave their Facebook page. Talk about a great user experience!"

What HubSpot liked:

"Shopify is an e-commerce website platform, and a prolific multimedia publisher, evidenced by its Facebook page. Whilst its photos section consists of branded infographics that share data from the industry, its video section is full of how-to clips you'd normally see in article form."

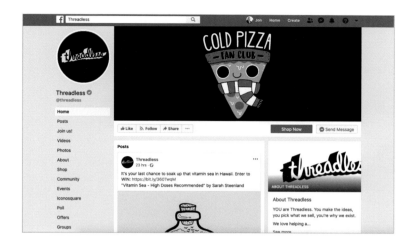

What HubSpot liked:

"Threadless has tons of great images on their Facebook page. Most notably, their constantly changing cover photo features different T-shirt designs. They also carry over important functionality from their website, including a "Shop Now" tab where you can begin browsing for a particular product.

All in all, Threadless does a great job of creating a fantastic user experience that doesn't require the user to leave Facebook. Plus, they have a badge in their "About" section signifying that they respond to inquiries quickly – which is great for showing fans and followers that they're listening."

Make Facebook work for you

If you have a pinch of creative flair and you are able to build a community, then Facebook will work for your business. From personal experience there are a few industries that have failed on Facebook, and these are mainly from the legal and financial industries.

Now it is your turn. Work through the rest of the chapter and see if you pass the 10-point checklist at the end of this chapter for your own Facebook page.

Creating your Facebook account

Before you can create a Facebook business page, you must first create your personal Facebook account.

To create your personal account:

 Visit **www.facebook.com** and complete the online registration process.

 When you've finished the registration process you'll be sent an email. Click the link in the email to verify your account.

To create your business page:

1 Visit **www.facebook.com/pages**

2 Follow the setup procedure, choosing your category carefully as this will decide your page features.

3 Complete all areas of your business page, as explained in the following pages of this chapter.

Assigning page roles
Even if you're a sole trader, it's always worth giving a trusted friend or family member a page role so that they can make updates or changes on your behalf. To do this:

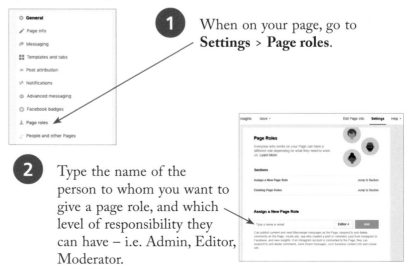

1 When on your page, go to **Settings** > **Page roles**.

2 Type the name of the person to whom you want to give a page role, and which level of responsibility they can have – i.e. Admin, Editor, Moderator.

Beware

You won't be able to progress to set up a business page until you've verified your personal account.

Don't forget

You will need to be logged in to your personal profile first as this determines your permissions to edit/update your Facebook business page.

About

It cannot be stressed enough how important it is to have a completed "About" area on your Facebook business page, so check to make sure that all areas are complete. There are always key areas that are often missed; therefore, we will walk you through these steps.

The first habit to develop when running a business page on Facebook is the function known as "switching". When you log in to Facebook, you will automatically log in as your personal profile.

"Switching" simply means clicking on the drop-down arrow, which is located to the right of your Facebook profile.

It is important to try to get used to Facebook language at this stage.

From here you will see a menu that takes you to your business page:

 Once you have "switched", then you need to access the admin area – click **About**.

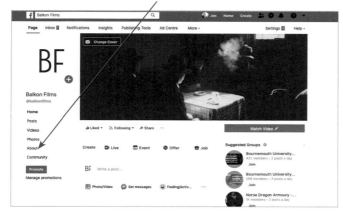

...cont'd

 Fill in the fields in the **About** area.

 Make sure that all areas are completed as much as possible.

Description/Categories

Take the time to complete these sections fully. The description of your page and the categories will determine how users who don't know your brand can find your page within the Facebook platform as well as through Google Search.

Phone number/Website/Email address

This isn't just useful information that will allow users to further investigate your brand and your offering; they act as ways to validate your business. Users who don't know you are thinking: "Are you real? Do you have a physical address, and if so, will that impact shipping costs?" (If you're selling physical products online.) "Can I find more about your brand or products on your website? If I want to contact you, what's the best email address to use?"

Hours

Some clients will want to visit you. By advertising your hours you show willingness to receive visitors, but this also sets expectations on how quickly they can expect a reply to any questions or comments they may send.

Impressum/Products/Privacy Policy

An Impressum page is used to display information about your company such as the name/s of the directors, registered address, and the legal status of the business entity, such as a limited company. In certain countries such as Germany, it is a legal requirement to include this information. In the Products section you have the opportunity to further list and explain your product offering, which is great for search, both on the Facebook platform but also a wider Google search. Lastly, a Privacy Policy allows the opportunity for you to reassure users of your commitment to privacy.

Do you have a fully completed "About" area? If you can answer "yes" to this question, then give yourself a point.

Grabbing your unique URL

When you register your company page on Facebook, you are allocated a URL (website address). However, the original URL is not very attractive and has a long string of numbers after your page name, like this:

🔒 https://**www.facebook.com**/pages/Salon-Alchemy/209205155771759

Having a URL that is easy to remember so that you can add it to your business cards and letterheads, and tell it to people that you meet, is a real bonus. Therefore, you would like your Facebook URL (sometimes called a vanity URL or username) to look something like this:

🔒 https://**www.facebook.com**/outcasthairsalon

If you still have a URL for your page that has a long string of numbers after it, before you reach 200 likes on your business page you have the opportunity to create your own unique page name.

Follow these instructions to grab your unique URL for your Facebook page:

 Click on **Create Page @username**.

Don't forget

Remember – a "profile" is a person and a "page" is a business or organization.

2 Enter the username you would like to use and make your own. You have up to 50 characters. Note that you can't use spaces. As you type, the platform will give you real-time feedback as to whether that username has already been taken. You'll know your proposed username is acceptable when a green check mark appears. When you're happy with your choice, click **Create Username**.

Keep this username as short as possible.

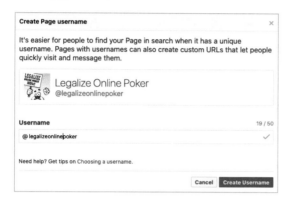

Here are a few key things to remember before you go ahead:

- You cannot claim a username that is already in use.
- Usernames are unique. Choose a username you'll be happy with for the long term. Usernames are not transferable, and you can only change your username once.
- Usernames can only contain alphanumeric characters (A-Z, 0-9) or a period/full stop (".").
- Periods/full stops (".") and capitalization don't count as a part of a username – for example, jonjones66, Jon.Jones66 and jon.jones.66 are all considered the same username.
- Usernames must be at least five characters long and can't contain generic terms.
- You must be Admin level to choose a username for a page.
- Make sure you're happy with your username (and double-check the spelling) before confirming it. Once you're sure you're happy, click **Confirm**.

Your old URL will redirect to the new one, so you don't need to worry about updating your previous links.

Do you have your unique username? If "yes", then you are awarded another point on the checklist at the end of the chapter.

Branding your Facebook page

We have all heard the famous quote: "You never get a second chance to make a first impression." What is your current Facebook page saying about your business? Here are the main areas in which you can brand your page:

The cover photo

This is your opportunity to show off your brand, and the cover photo is showcased loud and clear at the top of your page. This header-style image enables you to present your products, services and anything else that you wish to announce to the world.

Optimize your cover photo for the right dimensions: 820 pixels wide x 312 pixels tall for desktop; 640 pixels wide x 360 pixels tall for mobile. If your uploaded image is smaller than these dimensions, Facebook will stretch it to fit, making it look blurry.

Update your cover photo at least once every two months to keep your page fresh. When you upload a new cover photo it is also posted on your timeline, giving your page greater visibility, so ensure that you always add a description, including a link to your website. Adding a description should not be ignored. Unfortunately, you cannot add a description at the same time as uploading a cover photo. Here is the process for changing and uploading a new cover photo:

1 Hover over your cover photo with your mouse toward the top left-hand corner. You will then see a prompt appear: **Change Cover**.

Hot tip

Always add a description to your cover photos.

2 Click on **Change Cover**:

- **Choose from photos** – This gives you the option to select from a previously uploaded cover photo.
- **Choose from videos** – This gives you the option to select from a previously uploaded video.
- **Upload photo/video** – This gives you the option to select an image or video from your desktop or mobile device.
- **Edit slideshow** – This gives you the opportunity to change a previously created slideshow.
- **Remove** – If you click this option, then you are left with a blank cover photo (not recommended).

For this exercise, let's explore the third option: Upload photo.

3 Select from your images the photo that you would like to upload. Remember that it needs to be a minimum of 400 pixels wide. Double-click your image.

4 Use the **Drag to reposition** area until the image sits perfectly on your page, then click **Save** when you are happy.

...cont'd

A professionally designed cover photo can do wonders for your brand, and you can use it every year, so you only need it designed once.

5 Once you have saved the changes, then you need to add a description (this is the magic ingredient that helps with Google Search, and will also encourage people to comment on your new cover photo). Click anywhere on the cover photo to access the area where you can add your description.

Adding as much detail as you can, including a link to a specific product or service, is ideal. Once you have completed this area in full, click **Finished Editing** and you are good to go.

Change your cover photo at least once every two months.

Image (c) Bert Hardy - Chinese Seamen, Liverpool, 1942

Who were you with?

Liverpool

🌐 Public   **Finished Editing**   Cancel

👍 1

👍 Like   💬 Comment   ↪ Share   BF ▼

BF   Comment as Balkon Films   ☺ 📷 GIF 🙂

Press Enter to post.

Why not try some themes for your cover photos? Here are some examples of other themes that work well throughout the year:

- New Year
- Shrove Tuesday (Pancake Day)
- St Patrick's Day
- Mothering Sunday
- April Fools' Day
- Tennis, Grand Prix, Cricket, and other major sporting events
- Thanksgiving
- International Day of Charity, Comic Relief, Sports Relief, and other charity events
- Father's Day
- Summer time
- Back to School
- Bonfire Night
- Hallowe'en
- Christmas

Plan your cover photo designs throughout the year.

...cont'd

The avatar/profile photo

What is the right Facebook profile photo size in 2020? In 2020, the ideal Facebook profile photo size is 360 x 360 pixels. But Facebook profile photos must be at least a minimum size of 180 x 180 pixels. The optimal size for a Facebook cover photo is 828 x 465 pixels.

In my opinion, the avatar or profile photo is probably the most important image on your page, because it appears in so many places as well as next to your cover photo, including:

The newsfeed of your followers

You should be designing your profile picture for THAT location. It is great to have fancy profile images that work alongside your cover photo, but if it does not work in the newsfeed then you need to scrap the idea and start again. You need to ask yourself: Is my brand recognized in the newsfeed?

Hot tip

Make sure your profile picture fits in the space provided.

Don't forget

If your logo is not visible in the newsfeed, then change your profile picture.

Posts on your page's timeline

Every time you post on your timeline, or reply to a comment, it is your avatar/profile picture that is displayed.

Comments and posts you make on other pages while using your page

Given that your avatar will be next to each and every post and comment, you can see how important a strong avatar is if you're keen on letting other businesses know about your brand. If the logo does not fit correctly, it looks stretched or truncated, or if it's been reduced so much you are unable to read it on the timeline, then not only are you missing a valuable brand awareness opportunity, but you're devaluing your brand in the eyes of potential and existing customers who will make a judgment call about you and your products based on this image alone.

Tips for creating a great-looking profile picture that your audience will recognize immediately:

- Use your logo if you have one.
- Minimize or eliminate all text if possible.
- If you are a business or brand, don't use a headshot, unless you are your brand.
- Do not change it very often, as consistency is the name of the game here (but change your cover photo regularly).
- Use an image that is recognizable and consistent with your other social networking platforms.
- Never, ever use stock photos.
- Make sure it's square (which I appreciate is easier said than done for some businesses).

How to produce excellent content

When it comes to content on your page, it is best to adhere to the Pareto Principle, otherwise known as the 80/20 rule.

Wikipedia explanation:

The distribution is claimed to appear in several different aspects relevant to entrepreneurs and business managers. For example:

- *80% of a company's profits come from 20% of its customers*
- *80% of a company's complaints come from 20% of its customers*
- *80% of a company's profits come from 20% of the time its staff spend*
- *80% of a company's sales come from 20% of its products*
- *80% of a company's sales are made by 20% of its sales staff[9]*

Therefore, many businesses have an easy access to dramatic improvements in profitability by focusing on the most effective areas and eliminating, ignoring, automating, delegating or retraining the rest, as appropriate.

Implementing this rule into social media and Facebook content marketing:

20% of everything that you post onto Facebook should be "branded content". This means content that will educate your audience about your products, your service, your brand, etc. Below is an example of 20% content.

Abide by the 80/20 rule at all times and you can't go wrong.

20%

Events

Features of your services

Links to your blog

Tips on your industry

Promoting special offers

Benefits of your products

Links to "meet the team"

This content will attract a number of likes, comments and shares.

But Facebook is a SOCIAL network, with an emphasis on the word "social".

Only people that interact and engage with your posts will see your content (unless you pay for Facebook advertising). Therefore, 80% of your posts should be to encourage conversation from your audience.

Here are some examples of good posts:

- Open-ended questions.
- Fill in the blanks.
- Behind the scenes (is it someone's birthday in the office?).
- Quotes.
- Quizzes – guess the object.
- Trivia.
- Welcoming people to your page.
- Family and pets.
- Videos and tips.
- Funny/humorous.
- Pictures from events or trade fairs.
- Seasonal posts.

It is worth noting that Facebook frowns upon "like-baiting". Like-baiting is when you ask for comments, likes and shares within the post. Facebook knows that you are trying to manipulate the system.

A few examples of a "like-baiting" post would be something like:

By a show of LIKES, how many people would dress up their pets with Holiday reindeers?

[First Sunday in Feb] It's Super Bowl Time! Will it be [team] or [team]? Tell us in the comments!

Click LIKE if the first site you go to in the morning is Facebook... leave a COMMENT if not and tell us the first site you go to.

These types of posts are big no-nos!

Adding milestones

Adding milestones to your business page is a great way to promote your company's history and showcase your achievements.

How do you add a milestone to your page?
To add a milestone for your business, you must be logged in as your page.

 Click on the ellipsis/three dots to the right of **Liked | Following | Share.** You will see a drop-down menu.

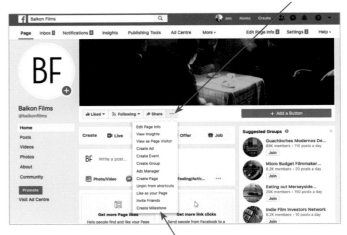

 Click on **Create Milestone** to record a company/business milestone on your timeline.

Don't worry if you decide you want to add milestones long after the actual date the event occurred. It's possible to backdate your posts. Also, by adding a series of historical milestones you won't flood your timeline. If you post a milestone for 1989, then it will appear in your timeline for 1989, rather than the date that you posted it.

Ensure that you complete all relevant areas of the milestone page for maximum impact, including images and a story to support the event. Here's your opportunity to explain why the event was so significant for your business, mention the members of staff or teams who were critical in reaching the milestone and, if relevant, the customer or client who helped you get there (i.e. 1,000th customer).

Once you complete the milestone information and click **Save**, the milestone will appear as a post on your timeline. Because it's a milestone, the size of the post is slightly larger than a regular post and it includes the milestone star–animated GIF, which helps to draw attention to your milestone.

Some ideas of milestones for your business could be:

- When your business was established.
- When new locations are opened.
- Staff promotions.
- Working with a new sector.
- When you establish important partnerships.
- Brand new website.
- When you have gained important accreditations.
- When you receive awards or recognitions.
- Launch of new products or services.
- Celebrating numbers of likes.
- Welcoming new staff.
- Significant customer wins or number of customers.

Do you have milestones added to your Facebook page? If you have more than four milestones, then give yourself a point.

Connecting Facebook with Instagram

Connecting Facebook with Instagram will allow you to both respond to comments and messages and create advertisements for Instagram on Facebook.

1 Within Settings, click on **Instagram** in the left-hand panel to connect your Facebook account with your Instagram account by clicking **Connect Account**.

Adding a call-to-action button

Adding a call-to-action (CTA) button will encourage page visitors to take an action from your page, such as shop or sign up.

1 Click **Add a Button**.

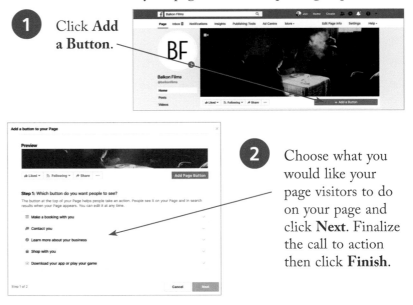

2 Choose what you would like your page visitors to do on your page and click **Next**. Finalize the call to action then click **Finish**.

Conclusion

In conclusion, having a Facebook page can be very rewarding for a business. Let's look at the four steps to Facebook success:

 Build your platform

If you have branded your Facebook business page, added milestones, grabbed your URL, completed all the information in the "About" area, then you should be confident in saying that you have reached stage one of Facebook success for a business owner.

 Grow your network

Start posting and commenting on the posts of others to get started with growing your network. Add a link to your Facebook page within the signature of your email correspondence and, if you have a physical shop or office your clients can visit, be sure to encourage them to like your page. Very quickly you will have reached a reasonable number of likes for your page, and you will have reached stage two of Facebook success for your business.

3 **Implement a strategy**

Begin testing what time of day is best for engagement with your target market. Is your key audience online mornings, noon, or night? Have you started to add hashtags to your posts and are you now mixing up the content you share in posts? If you're now posting a healthy mix of images, videos, opinions on news articles, customer testimonials, and "behind the scenes" posts about your team or staff, then well done! You have now achieved stage three of Facebook success for a business owner.

4 **Measure the results**

There are many ways in which to measure the results for Facebook, but the easiest way is to use Facebook Insights, which can be found in the Insights tab along the top toolbar of your Facebook business page. Products such as Hootsuite (see page 220) and other software can also produce statistics for you. If you measure your results, tweak your strategy and then measure again the following month, then give yourself a pat on the back as you have reached stage four of Facebook success for a business owner.

Checklist

It's time to be totally honest now and have a look at your score for your Facebook page.

 Is your "About" area completed in full?

 Have you assigned "page roles" to other members of staff?

 Have you grabbed your unique URL?

 Have you branded your cover photo and profile picture/avatar?

 Have you added your address and hours of operation?

 If your page has some great content with a variety of images, videos, and text posts, as well as a mix of 20% content and 80% type of content, then please award yourself a point for content.

 Do you have four or more milestones on your page?

 Is your page name searchable?

 Have you connected your Facebook page with Instagram?

10 Have you added a call-to-action button?

One could write a whole book on Facebook, but the above checkpoints are really a good starting point for all small business owners. How did you score out of 10?

12 Twitter

Introduction

If you are new to Twitter, then you may be wondering what all the fuss is about. Can it really help business owners achieve more sales, gain credibility, and create brand awareness, or is it just a waste of time? Here are seven reasons why you should be using Twitter if you are a business owner:

Don't forget

Twitter is a fast way to publish your message AND get instantaneous engagement.

1 **More people are using Twitter**
The local corner shop owner; the landscape gardener; accountants; solicitors; the local golf club; the job seeker; the property hunter – all sorts of people use Twitter, along with hundreds of large corporate companies who will be advertising their tender opportunities, and so much more.

Having your business on Twitter is popular, and you will be amazed how many opportunities you could be missing by not being a part of this world. If you are a local business, and perhaps you are already attending business-networking breakfasts such as BNI (Business Networking International), FSB (Federation of Small Businesses) or business lunches, then Twitter is certainly not a platform to ignore.

2 **The "cool" factor**
Using Twitter is evidence that your business is participating in this whole social media thing, and is obviously a "with-it" company that people might be interested in doing business with. It's not enough to just have a website nowadays.

3 **A fast way to get your message published**
Assuming your potential and existing customers are on Twitter, you can instantly let them know your news, whether it's an announcement of a new product, a special deal, or an upcoming event they may be interested in.

4 **Keep updated with industry news**
Twitter lets you hear what other people are saying. Using Twitter Search or their Advanced Search, you can find out what people are saying about a particular topic, enabling you to keep your ear to the ground about your company and, of course, your competition.

Enhance your brand awareness

By participating in Twitter (that is, using it to communicate with others, rather than just spamming product announcements and constantly broadcasting), you can present and develop the kind of image that attracts your potential clients. (Remember: communication is a two-way dialogue, not a monologue.) Branding of your Twitter account is discussed on pages 203-205.

Twitter opens opportunities to speak to high-profile people/companies

Being on Twitter will give you opportunities to meet and talk to an unlimited number of people, some of whom you would never get the chance to talk to otherwise. And some of those people might be the very business contacts you've been seeking: people you want to start projects with, source products from, or even recruit for your business.

The perfect tool for customer retention

Posting information about your products and/or services is the obvious use. But Twitter also gives you another channel for listening to and finding out about your customers – what they like or dislike about you or your company; how they feel about your brand; what suggestions they have for improvement; what their favorite products are and why... all kinds of nuggets that you can use to make your business more successful.

Twitter can provide your business with another channel to inform and engage your current and potential customers – and every opportunity to do that is worth exploring.

Creating your Twitter profile

Before you launch yourself into Twitter, you must first abide by stage one to social media success and build your platform (see page 153). Twitter is the easiest of platforms to create a profile for, as the information you need to provide is very limited.

To create your Twitter profile:

 Visit **www.twitter.com** and complete the online prompts.

 When registering your account you do not need to "follow" all the people as prompted; simply click on the X on each suggested person if you would rather not follow at this point.

 During the online registration process always check your location, as the default can be a random location. This is found in the Edit profile area.

Do not protect your tweets as this limits your visibility.

 You will be sent an email to verify the account – make sure you click on the link to confirm your Twitter account.

You can change your username at any time.

The 10 key elements of how to build your Twitter account, and the tools and techniques that can help enhance your Twitter presence, are illustrated in the following pages. As you go along, tick the boxes in the checklist at the end of the chapter and see what your score is.

Branding your Twitter account

You don't have to be a big brand like Pepsi or Virgin Media to brand your Twitter account, so take a look at the two main areas in which you can brand your Twitter account.

The avatar (profile picture)

The principles for branding your avatar are simple. Depending on the type of business you're in, either use a photo of yourself or a company logo. If you decide to add a company logo, then ensure that it fits correctly and it is not too "busy". This is the part of your brand that will communicate with other Twitter users throughout the day.

Square logos or head and shoulder photos work much better than rectangular logos.

Twitter avatar/profile picture

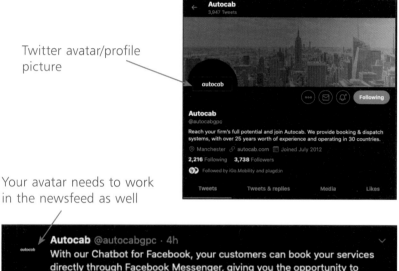

Your avatar needs to work in the newsfeed as well

Your Twitter profile picture size should be at least 400 x 400 pixels, and maximum 2MB. The file format should be JPG, PNG or GIF. Bear these sizes in mind when creating a Twitter avatar.

Does your avatar work? If you have a logo that is very long, it is very difficult to incorporate it into a profile picture. Look at creating a revised version of your logo, be it a symbol or even initials that work for Twitter.

…cont'd

To change your Twitter profile picture

 Click on **Edit profile**

 Click on the camera icon to change your profile image

 Select a new profile picture and upload the photo

The Twitter header

The Twitter header is an exceptionally important feature, as this is one of the main branding elements that appear on smartphone applications.

Header

Don't forget

Your Twitter header can be an aspirational image, your logo, an image of staff, your offices, or a product or service promotion.

Header Image: Twitter recommends dimensions of 1,500 pixels in width x 500 pixels in height

To change your Twitter header:

 Click on **Edit profile**

 Click the camera icon to change your header image

3 Select your image from your computer and then upload the photo

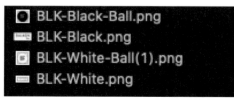

What does your Twitter account say about you? Does your avatar work well? Is your header branded and consistent with all other platforms online? If "yes", then congratulations! You are awarded a point in the checklist at the end of this chapter.

A healthy follower/following ratio

There is only one reason why some Twitter users follow hundreds of people, and that is simply to increase the number of people who follow them back. It is very easy to get large numbers of Twitter followers if you use this tactic, but quality far outweighs quantity every time.

Here are three reasons why following everyone back is a pointless task:

Twitter spam

I joined Twitter in 2009, and in those early days I was keen to get hundreds of followers as quickly as possible. All the blog articles I read were encouraging me to follow people – up to an additional 100 people every day – so that is what I did. Yes – I soon got into the hundreds quite quickly, but with this came additional work for me.

With Twitter, if you follow someone, you are giving that person the green light to send you a DM (direct message). Every day I was receiving spam messages: "Follow our Facebook page"; "Have you checked out our website?"; "Buy the latest gadget"; etc. It got to a point where I simply had to unfollow lots of people, and risk the chance that my own following might decrease – which it did.

The question I needed to ask myself was: if people are only following me because I am following them, does that mean that they are not really interested in the content that I am providing? Is it just a numbers game? From mid-2009, I made the decision to ONLY follow people that I am genuinely interested in talking to. Yes – I may not have thousands and thousands of followers, but I know that the people who are following me are genuinely interested in the content that I am providing, and this far outweighs the value of having thousands of followers who are not listening to anything I am tweeting.

Missing important tweets

Picture the scene: You are following 1,700 people. Your newsfeed is manic and full of noise. You log in to Twitter twice a day. How on earth do you keep in touch with the people that really count – your target market? You may be using lists (hopefully you are – see pages 210-214) to manage the people that you are following, but if you are following people who you have no intention of communicating with, then what's the point of following them?

Beware

The more people you follow, the more you are open to Twitter spam.

...cont'd

Twitter will tell you off

If you use the tactic of "follow loads of people so that they follow me back", then you will not be seen favorably in Twitter's eyes.

This account is suspended.

This account is currently suspended and is being investigated due to strange activity.

If this is your account, or for more information about why an account

Beware

If your ratio of followers is substantially lower than your following, then Twitter will suspend your account.

If you are not yet convinced that this is NOT a good method of increasing your Twitter followers, then here is an extract from Twitter's rules:

Twitter's technical follow limits

● *We don't limit the number of accounts you can follow overall, but there are some limits as to the pace at which you can do so.*

● *Every Twitter account is able to follow up to 400 accounts per day. Verified Twitter accounts are able to follow up to 1,000 accounts per day.*

● *In addition to the daily limits, there are follow ratios that go into effect once you're following a certain number of accounts: Every Twitter account can follow up to 5,000 accounts. Once you reach that number, you may need to wait until your account has more followers before you can follow additional accounts. This number is different for each account and is automatically calculated based on your unique ratio of followers to following.*

For more information, check out:
https://help.twitter.com/en/using-twitter/twitter-follow-limit

...cont'd

Make sure that you have a healthy follower/following ratio
Take advice from the celebrities. If you look at any of their
accounts, you will notice that the number of followers will far
supersede the number of people that the individuals are following.

This handy chart provided by **Follows.com** shows a number of
examples of Twitter accounts in which there are examples of an
unhealthy follower/following ratio. You can see in the fourth
example that the account initially appears quite vibrant, with
186,000 followers. However, looking at the volume of people
being followed (109,000) along with the sheer quantity of tweets,
it makes you wonder how many of those people are actually
listening to anything that is being tweeted here, or is it just a
numbers game?

TWEETS	FOLLOWING	FOLLOWERS	
11K	1,136	935	Follower/Following Ratio < 1
13.2K	10.2K	24.2K	Follower/Following Ratio > 1, but Following too many users
33.4K	474	2,179	Follower/Following Ratio > 1, and seems like a high quality account
109K	109K	186K	Follower/Following Ratio > 1, but Following too many users, and too many tweets
1,384	2,439	2,508	Follower/Following Ratio > 1, new account, playing follow/unfollow games
70.9K	509K	552K	Follower/Following Ratio > 1, following way too many accounts
20.3K	191	2,020	Follower/Following Ratio > 1, high quality account, popular users and content creators
2,652	5	192K	Follower/Following Ratio > 1, very high quality account, thought leader/celebrity

You will see in my own example Twitter account, there is a
healthy follower/following ratio. I have 427 followers but I am
only following
101 people, which
suggests that a
greater number of
people are following
me because they
are interested in
the content I am
tweeting out to the
world. Crucially, they
are not following my
account because I
am following them
back.

...cont'd

Celebs always have the best ratio, and you can see from Alan Sugar's Twitter account that he has over 5 million followers, but he is only following a mere 2,695 people.

It is worth noting that if an account has a tick next to the name, this represents a genuine and authentic account, and it is awarded by Twitter itself – this is not something that you can request to be added. To find out more about verified accounts, visit **http://www.twitter.com/help/verified**

If you follow hundreds or thousands of people, then your newsfeed will be very noisy!

Verified account

Creating Twitter lists is the easiest way to manage your account on a daily basis.

You do not need to actually "follow" people to put them on a list. Consider this when creating a list for your competitors.

Using Twitter lists

Twitter lists are underutilized. It is difficult to imagine how a user can follow more than 100 people without using Twitter lists. How would you keep on top of who is saying what in one long newsfeed, without being on Twitter 24/7?

Twitter lists are a great way to organize who you are following (and even who you are NOT following) into groups defined by you.

Here are examples of some of the Twitter lists:

Competitors (private list) – Set up a list of your competitors. You do not have to follow these accounts – just add them to your list. (Unless you have a good relationship with them and you would like to communicate with them.)

Clients (private list) – It is important to make sure that you do not miss any key notices or tweets from your existing clients.

Target market (public list) – For example, if you are a supplier to the wine industry, then you may want to have a list for all those potential clients who might be interested in your products. Following vineyards and wine merchants, and having these in one list, will keep you focused on your target market.

Press (public list) – Following local press, or perhaps national news, trade magazines, journalists, bloggers in an industry, etc. is always a good source of content ideas for your Twitter account, and is worthy of a list.

Famous (public list) – You may want to follow particular sporting personalities or business gurus, etc. I follow a number of thought leaders in my industry, and I have added these to my "Famous" list. I do not check this list every day but I know it is there, and I check on it a few times a week just to make sure that I do not miss anything important.

How do you create a Twitter list?
As with most platforms, there is always more than one way to achieve the same result, and creating a Twitter list is no exception, but here is an easy way to create those all-important Twitter lists:

1 Log in to your Twitter account. Click on the avatar on the far right-hand side and then click **Lists**.

2 Click on the **Create a list** button.

3 Name your list so that it is easily recognized. Complete the description (although this is not always necessary), and then select if this should be a private list (visible to yourself only) or a public list (visible in the public domain for all Twitter users to view and follow). Click **Save list**.

Do not create a public list of your clients.

How do I add people to my list?
Put ALL of the people that you are following into a list.

Visit **https://twitter.com/following**, which will give you a list of all the people that you are currently following.

...cont'd

1 Enter a name or part-name into the Search box.

2 Click **Add or remove from lists**.

Select which account you would like to add to your list by clicking on the profile image or name. If you accidentally add an account you do not want in your list, then click the **X**.

Develop a habit of adding to your list

Each time you follow a new person then add them to a list. Follow = add to list. If they are not worthy of being added to a list, then you may need to question yourself as to why you are following them in the first place.

How do you know if you've been put on a list?

It is nice to know when you have been added to a list. However, you will only notified if you have been added to a public list. To find out if you have been added to a private list, follow these steps:

1 Click on **Lists** in the left-hand menu.

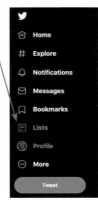

Check regularly if you have been put on any new Twitter lists.

...cont'd

There are three types of lists:

- **Owned**: Lists you've created yourself and have added profiles to.
- **Subscribed**: Public lists you've elected to subscribe to.
- **Member**: Private lists to which you've been added.

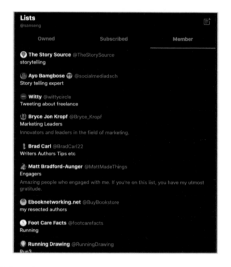

 Click on **Member** to see if you've been added to any lists.

Click on any of the lists to be taken through to all the tweets curated from members of that list. As you can see in the above example, my profile has been added to a number of lists that center around writing, storytelling, marketing, and running.

If you are using the Twitter application on your smartphone, then you will see in the notification area when someone has added you to a public list. However, at the time of writing this book, you are not currently able to receive these as push notifications.

...cont'd

Deploy the "notice me" strategy

One of the main strategies that we deploy at Autocab is called the "notice me" strategy, which involves the use of Twitter lists.

Set up a "notice me" list on Twitter. On this list you should only have a maximum of 10 key accounts. These are your key prospects that you would like to engage with, and ultimately you would like them to follow you back. Each day your objective is to engage with the people in the list. Perhaps re-tweet them one day, mention them in a tweet on occasions, and generally make yourself present and visible without annoying them.

If you're taking the time to build a good relationship with a Twitter user, and often re-tweeting their articles to your network or saying nice things about them, they will consider following you back over a period of time. Once a person in this list follows you back, they get removed from the list and added to a different list. Then, you add your next prospect. The key is to be specific, and to make sure that you have no more than 10 people in this list at any one time.

> **If you are following over 100 people, do you have Twitter lists created? If so, then congratulations – you are awarded a point in the chart at the end of this chapter.**

Using hashtags

If you're a Twitter novice, hashtags – those short links preceded by the hash sign (# – otherwise known as a pound sign) – may seem confusing and pointless. But they are integral to the way we communicate on Twitter, and it's important to know how to use them.

On Twitter, the hash sign (or pound sign) turns any word or group of words that directly follow it into a searchable link. The easiest way to describe it is, similar to writing a website address, or an email in a document, it will automatically turn blue. You then know if you click on the blue word, it will automatically send you to the site. Putting a hashtag in front of a word on Twitter will have a similar effect. If you type #DigitalMarketingUK then you will see everyone who is tweeting about digital marketing specifically in the UK, and you can join in the conversation.

Here is the Wikipedia description of a hashtag:

> "A hashtag… is a type of metadata tag used on social networks such as Twitter and other microblogging services. It lets users apply dynamic, user-generated tagging that helps other users easily find messages with a specific theme or content."

Keep in mind that the @ symbol does something completely different.

Using @ before a person's Twitter name will tweet that person directly, letting them know you have written to them via the @ connect feature. A hashtag will not. I will often see messages that say #sanseng, which is picked up by my listening software, when someone really should have used @sanseng instead. If you are trying to contact someone direct, then do not use the hashtag.

You may think that there is a whole list of hashtags somewhere, but in reality there is no preset list of hashtags. Create a brand new hashtag simply by putting the hash before a series of words, and if it hasn't been used before, then you can do a little dance! You've invented a hashtag!

Warning! If you are running an event, then make sure that you check out the hashtag to see if anyone is using it before you announce it to the world. (Just enter the hashtag into the Twitter Search facility to see if anyone else is tweeting using this hashtag.)

Beware

Using a hashtag in front of someone's name on Twitter will not notify the individual of the tweet.

...cont'd

I once ran a conference for over 400 recruiters, utilizing a specific hashtag, only to find that on the very same day, the hashtag was also being used by a ladies' bodybuilding event. Needless to say, the large screen at the conference displaying the Twitter hashtag wall was quite entertaining!

Are there any rules to using a hashtag?
I would highly recommend not using more than two or three hashtags in any one tweet, otherwise your message will start to reflect a list of keywords rather than an engaging message.

Refrain from hashtagging general words that will not be followed, such as #marketing #business. A hashtag is better used when you have something specific in mind, such as a location (town, city, country), industry jargon, or an event.

Here is an example of a bad use of hashtags. As you can see, the message is completely diluted as you are faced with an array of hashtagged words, which have no real meaning.

 #Design education by distance learning. We have trained students in 17 countries! #interiors #landscape #fashion #lighting #furnishing #CAD #DigitalLearning

Look at your last two weeks of tweets. Are you using hashtags? If the answer is "yes", are you using them in the right context? Congratulations – you have now gained another point in the checklist at the end of the chapter.

Never use any more than three hashtags in any tweet.

Using short URLs

There are many reasons to use a short URL, but first let me give you an example to illustrate what a short URL actually means.

In Twitter, you only have a maximum of 280 characters to get your point across (raised from 140 characters when Twitter first launched). If I wanted to tweet a link to a website, I would write:

> @sanseng Lead Generation Lesson 17 – Want to learn how to post a link in a tweet? Click here to find out how to make your tweets drive visitors to your site or blog: **https:// support.twitter.com/articles/78124-posting-links-in-a-tweet** #TwitterKnowledge #LearnTwitter #DriveTraffic

This tweet is 270 characters, and you can see that the link is dominating the message. If I was using a short URL tool, then it would look more like this:

> @sanseng Lead Generation Lesson 17 – Want to learn how to post a link in a tweet? Click here to find out how to make your tweets drive visitors to your site or blog: **http://ow.ly/ tHHKb** #TwitterKnowledge #LearnTwitter #DriveTraffic

This tweet is 221 characters in length, and leaves room for others to re-tweet my message to their audience, and add their own commentary. When Twitter users click on the short link, they will be directed to the long link above, achieving the same objective.

There are two main reasons why we recommend using shortened links in your everyday tweets:

They make links more manageable

Many website addresses that link to blog posts or articles are too long and wordy for SEO. One of Google's and other search engines' considerations with regard to SEO are keywords in the URL. This creates a problem for the user. The URLs help describe the content, but are lengthy and are not easy to share on emails, web pages, and especially social media platforms like Facebook, LinkedIn and, of course, Twitter.

URL shorteners help solve the problem of making links more manageable to share, and certain services allow users to add keywords to describe the link.

Use software to shorten your links so that others can easily re-tweet your message.

...cont'd

They can track and compile click data

There are over 100 different URL-shortening sites. However, here are three sites to get you started. Most of these sites will provide you with generous statistics:

https://tinyurl.com – TinyURL is customizable, but does not offer any form of tracking. Should you wish to use the shortened URL as part of an advertising campaign then **Bitly** is better suited. However, if you just want to shorten a long URL for a social media post, it's perfect.

https://bit.ly – Bitly is probably the most popular, as it saves a copy of the page linked to, tracks "conversations", and offers bookmarking features.

www.ow.ly – Part of the social media management suite called Hootsuite (see page 220). You do not need to be a user of this software to use the URL-shortening feature, but you do need to have a Twitter account. You are able to track a variety of statistics using Ow.ly, which is why we favor this particular software above all others.

As Twitter, general social media, and mobile internet are so popular, the need to make sharing web content easier should not be ignored. Shorter URLs are becoming more and more integral to that cause.

> **Are you using short URLs in your tweets? If so, are you measuring those results and learning from the stats? If "yes", then give yourself a point in the checklist at the end of this chapter.**

Social media management tools

Social media is one of the most effective ways for you and your business to get more traffic and generate new leads. Having a presence on all the major platforms like Facebook, Twitter, LinkedIn, Instagram, and Pinterest is a necessity these days for any business. But it is rather time consuming to manage all of these platforms, which is why most business owners who are serious about social media will use a social media management tool.

Never schedule tweets for appointments as this can get you into trouble.

Why use a social media management tool?
Scheduling your 20% content increases efficiency
Planning your social media, and then scheduling it into a social media management tool makes your life so much easier. If you abide by the 80/20 rule as mentioned in Chapter 11 – Facebook, then 20% of your posts can be planned and scheduled across multiple platforms from one place.

Beware, though. You could create all your tweets on a Sunday for the forthcoming weeks, including "thank you" messages for future meetings. However, if a meeting was canceled or rescheduled, you might forget to cancel the tweet, which could make you look a bit silly. So, only schedule your 20% content. The 80% should be live tweets.

You will increase your exposure to a larger target market
Engagement and communication are the most important goals to achieve in the Twittersphere. Sure, other metrics apply, but for the most part, if people are complimenting your content, they will share it. So, using a social media management tool allows you to see what your community is saying about your brand, product, or service. It's an amazing listening tool.

A better understanding of social media metrics
This is key for all social media marketers. What good are you as a marketer if you can't deliver a return for your social media marketing efforts? That is a great feature of many social media management tools. They provide you with reporting metrics and other data to help clarify if your efforts had an impact on your social communities.

...cont'd

Eliminate the possibility of spelling and grammar mistakes

All humans make mistakes – it is inevitable. However, there are ways to decrease the margin of error by taking advantage of social media marketing tools. By allowing you to post updates and content to multiple channels from one location, you can eliminate any typos or other publishing errors that would normally occur.

Which social media management tools work best for Twitter?

hootsuite.com

There are many social media management tools out there to choose from. However, Hootsuite is a great tool for managing Twitter and other social media accounts.

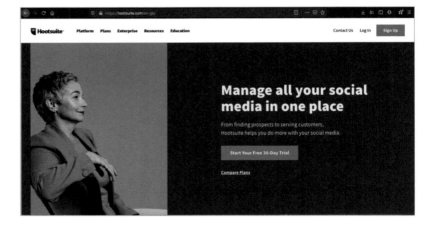

Hootsuite is a paid-for service that offers a range of price points to suit every budget. At the time of going to print, the cost of a professional account is $29 a month, which offers you one user account and up to 10 social profiles. There are enhanced plans that give you many more social profiles and many more users – perfect if you have a team looking after your marketing and social media. It is really worth every cent!

buffer.com

Buffer is a smart and easy way to schedule content across social media. Think of Buffer like a virtual queue you can use to fill with content and then stagger posting times throughout the

The Buffer app also provides analytics about the engagement and reach of your post.

day. This lets you keep to a consistent social media schedule all week long without worrying about micro-managing the delivery times.

socialoomph.com

SocialOomph is a web tool that provides a host of free and paid-for productivity enhancements for social media. There are lots of useful Twitter features like scheduling tweets, tracking keywords,

Some of the social media gurus such as Social Media Examiner use the functionality of SocialOomph, so it is well worth consideration.

viewing mentions and re-tweets, DM (direct message) inbox clean-up, auto-follow, and Auto-DM features for new followers.

tweetdeck.twitter.com

TweetDeck offers a "single view'" of your Twitter account – easily keep an eye on your feed, mentions, and direct messages, as well as your choice of hashtags.

Do not use the Auto-DM feature on SocialOomph for when someone follows you. It is impersonal and not a good Twitter strategy.

Do you manage your Twitter account using a social media management tool? If "yes", then give yourself a point in the checklist at the end of this chapter.

Content and engagement strategies

Hot tip

If your target market is very active on Twitter, then allocate a minimum of 30 minutes a day to your Twitter activities. (This is an ideal scenario – you'll be a better judge of the time you can spend on this exercise based on your other business activities.)

It is easy to become distracted when engaging in Twitter each day. Whilst it's important to track what's trending, which hashtags are getting traction, and which news items you do or do not want to associate with your brand, focus your time on staying relevant to Twitter users by tweeting promptly about the topics that will make a difference to your customers. If you find that there's simply too much noise, here are two techniques that can help:

Use Twitter lists and start talking to people

If you are using Twitter to simply broadcast your products, services, properties or jobs, then Twitter will not be a successful platform for you. Twitter is becoming a news facility to instantly receive information on industries and breaking headlines, but in reality, if you are a business owner then the top of your list should be "engage with your target market".

For example, if your target market is those businesses linked to the recruitment world, you could have a list called "Recruitment". If you can only allocate 30 minutes a day to your Twitter activities, then your Recruitment list is where you need to start. You can click on your list then re-tweet, share, mention, and communicate with the Twitter users that are in this list.

Block out the noise

There is a fantastic smartphone application called Tweetbot, which has a mute section and is extremely handy when you need to focus on pure conversation. You can launch Tweetbot when you want to talk to people who are tweeting real live information, not automated or scheduled posts.

To give you an idea, here is a quick list of keywords or platforms that I have muted:

- #job – as I follow lots of recruiters but I am not interested in a new job.
- Interesting article – as this word is also associated with scheduled tweets.
- Interesting blog.
- Blog archive.
- Thanks for the follow.
- Worth a read.
- Buffer – as all these tweets are automated and not live.
- Facebook – if a post is coming from Facebook, then I know that the person is not present on Twitter.
- Paper.li – an automated newspaper service.
- Scoop.it.
- SocialOomph.

It takes a while to figure out which keywords are worthy of being muted, but it's a great function that cuts out an awful lot of Twitter noise.

Tweet what you are up to today

Are you going to an event, or perhaps meeting a client or supplier? Maybe you are having a new kitchen fitted, or you are writing Chapter Four of your novel. Whatever you are doing today, then schedule your tweets throughout the day. Remember to @mention people or companies in the posts to maximize your efforts. Be real; be authentic. Add the human touch to your tweets and watch that interaction rise.

Conclusion

1 Build your platform

Have you built your Twitter account correctly? Have you branded your Twitter header to showcase your services? Have you included an avatar/profile picture that works well in the timeline? Have you set up your Twitter lists? If you can answer "yes" to all of the above, then congratulations – you have reached stage one of Twitter success for a business owner.

2 Grow your network

What is your follower/following ratio? Is it a healthy ratio? Are you implementing a "notice me" strategy to grow those important prospective clients? Do you have Twitter lists set up that you are focusing on each day? If you can confidently say that you are doing everything in your power to grow your network on Twitter, then congratulations – you have reached stage two of Twitter success for a business owner.

3 Implement a strategy

Are you writing your 20% broadcasting tweets and scheduling those in a social media dashboard such as Hootsuite or Buffer? Have you defined your target market and created specific lists in Twitter to engage with them? Are you following press or industry-specific Twitter accounts to enable you to share content? Have you decided how much time you are going to spend on Twitter each day? Have you experimented with the timings of your tweets and measured when your followers are online? Doing so will quickly reveal when to tweet your most important tweets for maximum impact.

If you feel that you are organized, and you have set your goals and objectives for Twitter, and you have considered the majority of the above questions, then congratulations – you are en route to a successful Twitter account.

4 **Measure the results**

The same as all marketing, it is important to measure your results – otherwise, how do you know if you are being successful? Since Twitter is very open, there is a vast number of statistics that you can measure, but the key is to make sure that you are heading in the right direction and communicating with your audience to achieve your set goals and objectives.

For example, your main objective may be to "drive traffic to my website". If so, then the key measurement will come from your Google Analytics (see Chapter 15) and the social source traffic. However, if your key objective is "customer retention", then you should be measuring the @mentions and conversational goals that your business is having online.

If you are using a social media management tool such as Hootsuite, TweetDeck, SocialOomph, etc., then they all offer statistics for your Twitter account. The object of running these reports is to learn from them, tweak your strategy, and try to increase the numbers the following month.

Checklist

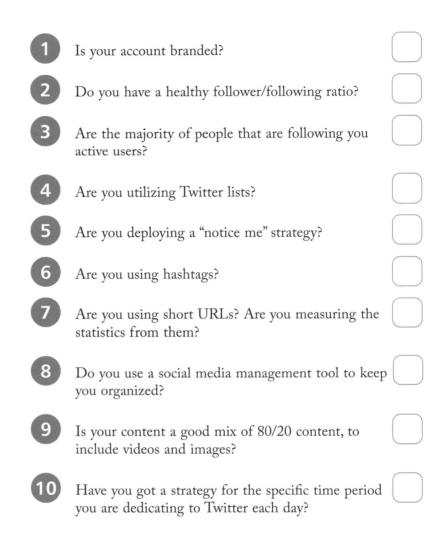

1   Is your account branded?

2   Do you have a healthy follower/following ratio?

3   Are the majority of people that are following you active users?

4   Are you utilizing Twitter lists?

5   Are you deploying a "notice me" strategy?

6   Are you using hashtags?

7   Are you using short URLs? Are you measuring the statistics from them?

8   Do you use a social media management tool to keep you organized?

9   Is your content a good mix of 80/20 content, to include videos and images?

10   Have you got a strategy for the specific time period you are dedicating to Twitter each day?

13 LinkedIn

So much more than an online résumé, LinkedIn is the largest professional social network in the world. Find out how to use LinkedIn to showcase your business, products and expertise.

An introduction to LinkedIn

LinkedIn is recognized more as a professional social networking site than other social networking platforms. If your target market is business-to-business (B2B), rather than business-to-consumer (B2C), then having a professional LinkedIn presence is a must. Some people feel that LinkedIn is becoming a place where job seekers and recruiters hang out, but it is so much more than that. Here are key reasons to use LinkedIn for your business:

- A great place to engage with and attract new potential clients.

- An excellent tool to source reliable suppliers.

- The ability to maintain top-of-mind awareness.

- One of the best and most effective ways to recruit new staff.

- The capacity to drive traffic to your website.

- The capacity to promote your products and services.

- The possibility of using it as a hub to collect testimonials and recommendations.

- The power to learn new skills and to be kept informed of industry news.

- The advantage of monitoring your competition.

- A great resource for gaining answers to tough business questions quickly.

- To promote customer retention and to nurture those existing client relationships.

Before you can set up your business or company page, you need to set up your personal profile if you don't have one. If you already have this in place, ensure it is up-to-date.

Visit **linkedin.com** and if you haven't already got a personal profile, follow the prompts to create one. Then, go through the following 20 steps to set up your profile.

20 steps to optimize your profile

First, you need to make sure your personal profile is completed correctly.

Click **Me** and then **View profile**

 Your name

Your name should only display your actual name. It is against LinkedIn rules to add telephone numbers, email addresses, symbols, or even LION (LinkedIn Open Networker – see "Don't forget" tip) after your name. To change your name, simply click the blue pencil icon.

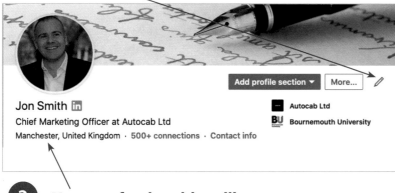

 Your professional headline

The default for your professional headline is your job title and company name. However, your professional headline is indexed by LinkedIn and also search engines. Therefore, you can also change your headline to display keywords within your industry.

To change your professional headline, click the pencil icon.

LION is an acronym for LinkedIn Open Networker. LIONs are LinkedIn members who are open to networking with everyone, irrespective of whether they know the people who have asked them to connect or not. The LION generally accepts every invitation request to connect or, at least, will not click the "I Don't Know This Person" button in response to an invitation.

Adding telephone numbers after your name is against LinkedIn rules and will eventually be deleted by LinkedIn.

...cont'd

Make sure that your avatar, more commonly known as your profile picture, is a professional image of you. Save your company logo for your company LinkedIn page.

Aim to have at least 501 connections on LinkedIn for social proof.

 3   **Your avatar/profile picture**

Refrain from adding a company logo, as this should be saved for your company LinkedIn page and not your personal profile. A professional head and shoulders image is ideal.

To add or change your profile picture, click the camera icon. The ideal LinkedIn profile picture size is 400 x 400 pixels. However, it's fine to upload a larger picture as long as it's square, no larger in file size than 8MB, and does not exceed 4,320 pixels in height or 7,680 pixels in width.

4   **Connections**

Your first goal should be to reach at least 501 connections for social proof, verification and excellent networking opportunities. When you are searching for contacts in the Advanced Search area, the results shown are the results from your network. If you have a larger network, then you automatically have better search results. (How to connect with people is shown later, on page 246.)

Your photo should always look professional

Your name should ONLY include your name. No numbers, no sales pitch, no LION

Your headline should be catchy and have keywords you would like to be found for

Connections

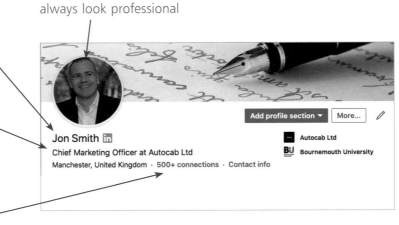

⑤ Add relevant contact information

This will include showcasing your company email. If you have set up your LinkedIn account with a Gmail/Hotmail/AOL etc. email, then that is fine, but you should add your company email to your LinkedIn account and consider making this the primary email that is displayed on your profile (see the Hot tip). Add additional information, such as your Skype name.

Click **Contact info**

You will then be presented with all of the contact information you have provided to LinkedIn. There is the opportunity to include website address/es, email addresses/es, your Twitter handle and Skype account – allowing potential clients to contact you in a number of different ways.

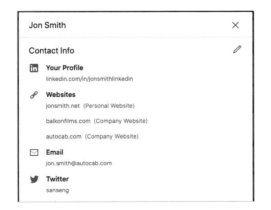

You can see from the example on page 232 that I have three email addresses on my LinkedIn account. I can log in to LinkedIn with any of these emails. However, I only showcase my company email.

Hot tip

If you are a sole trader you may prefer to use your company email address rather than your personal email address on your LinkedIn profile, otherwise you get all the contact request notifications and LinkedIn updates regarding posts, comments, and reactions to your personal email account rather than your company account. If you are an employee who is managing a company LinkedIn account you might also prefer to display your company email address for the same reason, as some firms don't allow staff to access their personal email account at work, so you wouldn't be able to see notifications during working hours.

Don't forget

An email must be verified before you can make it into a primary email. LinkedIn will email you a link, which you simply click to verify that the address exists.

...cont'd

Email addresses	Close
Add or remove email addresses on your account	3 email addresses

Email addresses you've added:

jon.smith@autocab.com		Primary
jon@jonsmith.net	Make primary	Remove
jon@balkonfilms.com	Make primary	Remove

You are allowed to add up to three websites on your LinkedIn company profile. It is highly recommended that you label your websites rather than selecting **Company Website**.

It is much more intuitive for the reader if you label your websites correctly so that they look more like this:

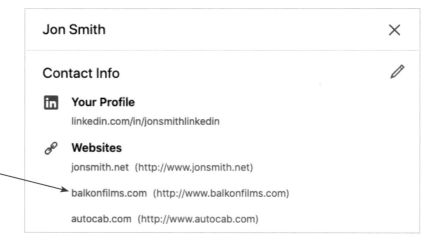
Jon Smith   ✕

Contact Info   ✎

🔗 **Your Profile**
linkedin.com/in/jonsmithlinkedin

🔗 **Websites**
jonsmith.net (http://www.jonsmith.net)

balkonfilms.com (http://www.balkonfilms.com)

autocab.com (http://www.autocab.com)

To label your websites: Click the pencil > Click **Other** > Give your website a label > Click **Save**

6   Edit your profile URL

Your original LinkedIn profile website address (URL) will be a mix of names and numbers and be unmemorable. To ensure that you have a clean-looking URL, which needs to be your name rather than a company name, edit your LinkedIn URL:

Click the blue **Edit pencil** next to your current URL, then enter the public profile URL of your choice

This should be your real name, or a variation of your name. If, like me, you have a very common name, it's quite possible that your first choice has been taken. Despite joining LinkedIn back in 2006 when it was a nascent platform, both Jon and Jonathan Smith had been taken by other users, so I added "linkedin" to my name to create something original and unique to me.

I would advise against adding your company name to your LinkedIn vanity URL for the simple reason that once this is set, it is set for life and cannot be altered, so choose wisely.

You can only edit your profile URL once. Therefore, make sure it is your name, rather than a company name.

...cont'd

7 Regularly update your activity

To stay in the minds of your clients and connections on LinkedIn, it is important to share regular content. Bear in mind that this is very much a business and professional network, so announcing to the world what you are having for breakfast today is not really something that you would share on this platform. Posting between one to five times a day seems to be an optimum number to have the most effect on a LinkedIn personal profile.

What kind of updates should you share on LinkedIn?
Here is a list of suggestions that may inspire you:

- Sharing a valuable article.
- Conversations that you may want to start.
- Information about an event you or your company are attending.
- Posting your blog articles.
- Posting your audio and video links.
- Announcing the networking event that you are attending and tagging in an individual or company that you are expecting to meet there.
- Adding tips or techniques about your industry or trade.
- Giving your opinion on trending topics or news headlines.
- Sharing your connections' content that may be relevant to your audience.

Sharing an activity update on LinkedIn

Click **Start a post** and share your thoughts...

Posting regularly is essential.

If you're looking to build your profile and extend your reach on LinkedIn, consider writing a longer-form article rather than a post. To do this, click on **Write an article**.

8 Use keywords in your summary

The summary of your profile is highly indexed by LinkedIn and search engines such as Google. Therefore, it is important to make sure that you have specific keywords within your summary.

There are many variations of summaries on LinkedIn profiles, and there really is no right or wrong way. Key points are:

- Do not make it too long (no more than five paragraphs).
- Add those keywords.
- Write in the first person (see Step 9 on page 236).

Hot tip

Do not write more than five paragraphs in your LinkedIn profile summary.

Hot tip

Use keywords that you would like to be found throughout the whole of your summary.

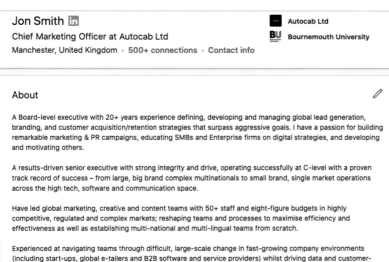

Jon Smith [in]
Chief Marketing Officer at Autocab Ltd
Manchester, United Kingdom · 500+ connections · Contact info

Autocab Ltd
BU Bournemouth University

About

A Board-level executive with 20+ years experience defining, developing and managing global lead generation, branding, and customer acquisition/retention strategies that surpass aggressive goals. I have a passion for building remarkable marketing & PR campaigns, educating SMBs and Enterprise firms on digital strategies, and developing and motivating others.

A results-driven senior executive with strong integrity and drive, operating successfully at C-level with a proven track record of success – from large, big brand complex multinationals to small brand, single market operations across the high tech, software and communication space.

Have led global marketing, creative and content teams with 50+ staff and eight-figure budgets in highly competitive, regulated and complex markets; reshaping teams and processes to maximise efficiency and effectiveness as well as establishing multi-national and multi-lingual teams from scratch.

Experienced at navigating teams through difficult, large-scale change in fast-growing company environments (including start-ups, global e-tailers and B2B software and service providers) whilst driving data and customer-focused product, process and operational improvements.

In my case, I am looking to summarize a 20+ year career in digital and e-commerce that has taken me around the world and has involved working for both small and large organizations at different stages of maturity. As a board director, I also have additional organizational skills beyond my own department.

My goal with this page is to give existing customers and potential clients the confidence that they're in good hands.

...cont'd

Write in the first person.

9 Write in the first person

This is your profile, which is written by you! Therefore, it does not read correctly if you have not written it in the first person. This is sometimes difficult to do, but your summary needs to read in an authentic light, perhaps up-selling key features of your business in the middle, and then showcasing some of your main achievements at the end.

10 Add rich text media to your profile

Adding rich text media (more commonly known as visuals) such as videos, PDFs, PowerPoint presentations, links, etc. to various parts of your LinkedIn profile is essential, and will take your profile to another level.

These areas are:

- Your summary.
- Experience (employment history).
- Education.

How do I add rich text media?

Simply click on the blue **Edit pencil**, and then select from **Upload** or **Link**:

Edit about   ✕

English (Primary profile)   Spanish

Summary

A Board-level executive with 20+ years experience defining, developing and managing global lead generation, branding, and customer acquisition/retention strategies that surpass aggressive goals. I have a passion for building remarkable marketing & PR campaigns, educating SMBs and Enterprise firms on digital strategies, and developing and motivating others.

Media
Add or link to external documents, photos, sites, videos, and presentations.

Upload	Link

In the example below, I have already added some rich media content to my current role.

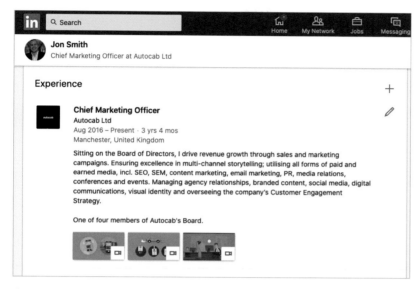

Some ideas that you may want to add as rich text media files are:

- A company brochure.
- An ebook.
- A PowerPoint or SlideShare presentation about your company.
- A company promotional video.
- A white paper.
- Fact sheets.

In my profile, I've added pertinent downloads or website addresses to each of my current/previous roles. In the case above, for Autocab, three short "explainer" videos give viewers a two-minute overview of some of our technical products.

This is a quick introduction to our services, in an easy-to-digest format for potential clients, which I believe is far more appealing than a long-winded company document or white paper.

...cont'd

11 **Add clear calls to action**

Once you have uploaded your rich text media, then add clear calls to action to each upload.

In this description, audiences understand it's a video and they're being persuaded to watch it because it points to specific business challenges taxi operators face; i.e. how to retain drivers and how to ensure a great level of customer service.

If you choose to add an ebook or white paper, give a brief summary in the description – why should people open and read this document, and what will they learn by doing so?

With a presentation, be sure to upload the PDF version of the slides – with more and more LinkedIn users accessing their pages via a tablet or phone, this will be far more effective than a PowerPoint or Keynote file.

12 ## Make the most of your skills and endorsements

Take a few minutes to make sure that your skills are listed correctly on your profile. If you do not yet have any endorsements on your key skills, then you can move them around so that the most important ones appear at the top of your list. (Just drag and drop.)

Click the link to add a new skill

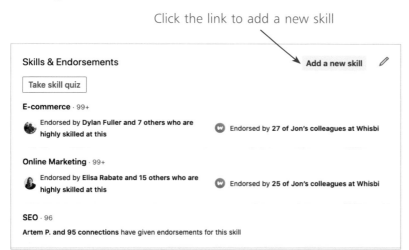

Start typing a relevant skill and then select from the drop-down menu or choose from the suggested skills:

Don't be shy! Celebrate what you're good at.

Always thank people for endorsing you.

If your skill set has not appeared in the drop-down menu, then simply click **Add** and it will create a new skill that others can also select in the future.

13 Update your projects

If you have not yet added projects to your profile, they can be found on the right-hand side, alongside certificates, languages, test scores, etc.

A project can be a stand-alone project you have completed as a freelancer, or it could be something that you conducted on behalf of the company you work for.

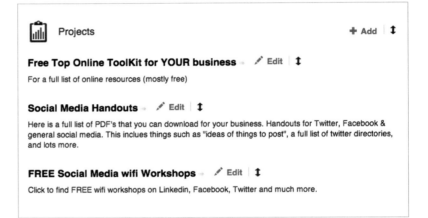

If you have resources such as white papers, brochures, case studies, etc. that people can download or link to, then this area is incredibly useful as another way to promote you, your company and your product or service. If the project was conducted at a specific time, include the dates:

Hot tip

Use the Projects section to highlight any free reports or downloads, or to showcase any products that you are promoting.

Beware

Only place items here that offer some value to your audience. Do not oversell!

14 ### Experience

Once again, your job title is indexed and appears on search engines. If you are a director of a company, then type **Director** but add some keywords about your business.

To edit your existing role, click on the blue Edit pencil icon

You may have more than one current job. The role with the latest start date first will be presented first.

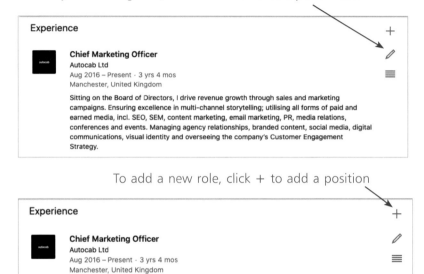

Experience   +

Chief Marketing Officer
Autocab Ltd
Aug 2016 – Present · 3 yrs 4 mos
Manchester, United Kingdom

Sitting on the Board of Directors, I drive revenue growth through sales and marketing campaigns. Ensuring excellence in multi-channel storytelling; utilising all forms of paid and earned media, incl. SEO, SEM, content marketing, email marketing, PR, media relations, conferences and events. Managing agency relationships, branded content, social media, digital communications, visual identity and overseeing the company's Customer Engagement Strategy.

To add a new role, click + to add a position

Experience   +

Chief Marketing Officer
Autocab Ltd
Aug 2016 – Present · 3 yrs 4 mos
Manchester, United Kingdom

Start typing the name of your company and select from the drop-down menu. Once you have selected your company, completed the relevant fields and clicked **Save**, the logo of the business will appear on your profile.

If the logo is not on your profile it signifies that the company was not selected from the drop-down menu, or that the owners of that page have not added the logo to the company page.

Add experience   ×

English (Primary profile)   Spanish

Title *
Ex: Retail Sales Manager

Employment type
-

Company *
Ex: Microsoft

...cont'd

15 Job description

Your job description will ideally be between three to four short paragraphs that have keyword-rich content. As you will see from the job description below, numerous keywords have been added that are relevant to the industries I work in such as "SEO", "content marketing", "social media", "digital communications", and "customer engagement", etc. Which keywords are relevant in your industry?

Add keywords in your job title

Add keywords within the job description. It will be picked up by Google!

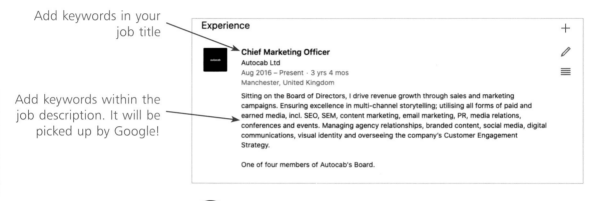

16 Recommendations

Make it part of your process to request a recommendation on your LinkedIn profile.

To request a recommendation, click **Ask for a recommendation** and then type in the name of whom you would like to ask

There is a limit of 200 recipients of a recommendation request that can be sent at any one time. It is worth noting that if you are requesting recommendations in bulk, then the email that arrives in the recipient's inbox will not be a group email; they are sent individually by LinkedIn.

Don't forget

You can only ask for a recommendation from LinkedIn members that are connected to you.

Recommendations   Ask for a recommendation ✏

Received (82)   Given (64)

Ian Tufts
CIO, CTO, COO - Helping organisations realise value through technology
February 13, 2019, Jon worked with Ian in the same group

Jon is an exceptional marketer. We worked together at Autocab and I was constantly impressed with his creativity and his innate ability to magically craft marketing material that was conveyed in a simple, yet compelling style. Jon never failed to amaze me how he always delivered on time, sometimes in the ... **See more**

You can send bulk recommendation requests. The recipients will not see other email addresses.

Recommendations are extremely important! Try to have at least 10. If you have fewer than 10, then make it your top mission!

17 Contact information

LinkedIn offers the opportunity for you to add contact information to your profile. Whilst it's a good idea to use this section to promote your business website address, business email address, and your business phone number, I would steer away from adding your home address, personal email, phone number, and birthday. If you have any concerns at all about your details being visible, leave the contact information blank, as prospects will still be able to contact you through LinkedIn Messaging or InMail.

18 Honors and Awards

Are you accredited with a governing body? Have you or your business won any awards? If so, then these may added here.

19 Limit how many groups to join

LinkedIn has capped the number of groups that you can join to 100. In any case, if you are actively involved in 100 groups each day then you will have very little time to run your business. Limit your groups and only spend time in the groups that are active and that you feel have some value, otherwise you may be wasting your valuable time and energy.

...cont'd

What are LinkedIn groups?

LinkedIn has created groups to foster collaboration and the sharing of best practice between individuals who may or may not be connected but share an interest in a particular theme.

Within groups, members can become involved in discussions relating to a particular industry or topic, and they are extremely popular on LinkedIn.

Groups can be closed and accessible to members only, or they can be open for anyone to join. Managing an active group can be quite time consuming, so take this into consideration if you are about to embark on that journey.

To join a group, click **Work** on the top navigation bar and then select **Groups**

Simply search for the keywords or the topic that you are interested in, and click **Join**

 20 **Showcase your groups on your profile**

On your personal profile it is important to show you're an active part of the industry in which you operate. By joining relevant groups you'll be exposed to others working and interested in the same areas as you – many of whom could become your future customers.

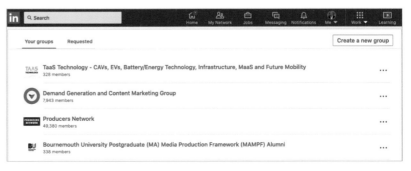

Hot tip

Do not sell or broadcast your company messages within a group. To be successful, you can add value by creating good topics of discussion.

By joining groups you will be exposed to the sort of content others are using to promote their businesses or products, which can prove to be useful when you're looking to build your own content pipeline.

Crucially, groups tend to be the place where the important conversations are taking place, and it's essential that **you** are part of that conversation too.

The popularity and usefulness of groups will ebb and flow as the months and years go by – largely down to the passion the group owner and members have for keeping the conversation going. Keep an eye on new groups that appear, and play an active role when and where you can.

And if there really isn't anything out there that does what you need it to do... then create your own!

Hot tip

Update your profile at least once every three months. It is amazing how things change. Put a date in your diary to remind you.

245

Connecting with people

You can ask people to connect with you on LinkedIn by sending them a personal invitation. Once they accept this invitation they will become a 1st-degree connection, and you will see a little "1st" in the top right-hand corner of their profile. If you see a "2nd" or "3rd", then this tells you that you are not yet connected.

You can invite people to connect with you from a variety of sources:

- **The People You May Know Page** – Viewed from the **My Network** button on the top toolbar.
- **The Connections page** – Viewed from the link in the left-hand panel.
- **A member's profile** – Simply click the **Connect** button on their profile.
- **Search results** – Click **Connect** to the right of the person's information.

To send out an invitation:

 Search for the person with whom you would like to connect, and click **Connect**.

 Personalize your invitation to connect by adding a note. By doing this, you will increase your chances of being accepted. If you met the person at a conference or event, mention that you've read something they posted, or you are connected to someone they are connected to.

You can customize this invitation

LinkedIn members are more likely to accept invitations that include a personal note.

Add a note   Send now

LinkedIn company page

There are many reasons why you should have a company LinkedIn page, but here are four key benefits:

- LinkedIn company pages are ranked by Google and highly indexed on LinkedIn.

- Providing a professional presence on one of the largest business networking sites.

- A great place to showcase the talents and skills of your team. This could be a freelancer who is happy to be associated with your business on LinkedIn, your co-directors, and staff.

- A place to showcase your company news, achievements and successes.

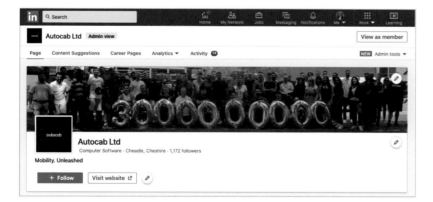

Let's take a look at how you can create your own company page.

Setting up a company LinkedIn page

Beware

A LinkedIn company page MUST be associated with a personal profile. It cannot be independent.

LinkedIn company pages have a number of different benefits compared with a LinkedIn personal profile, including visibility and education. Company pages help users learn about your business, brand, and job opportunities. Furthermore, the pages help users conduct their information search and evaluation.

Company pages help other users learn more about your business and the services you offer. By adding a company page, you can also educate them on the benefits of your products or services. Before you can create your own company page, you must have a personal LinkedIn profile. You must also ensure that your company doesn't already have a page on LinkedIn, and that you yourself meet the requirements to add a company page on LinkedIn.

To set up a LinkedIn page for your company, follow these steps:

1 Click **Work** and then click **Create a Company Page +** in the drop-down menu.

Choose the best option based on the number of employees:

 Complete the basic details required, tick the verification box and then click **Create Page**.

Once you have a basic page completed, here is a full checklist of everything else needed on your page.

How does your LinkedIn company page score in the following three-point check?

1 **Does your business page have a company cover photo?**

With exception to the avatar (company logo), the company cover photo is the first impression that you give of your company LinkedIn page. It is important to make sure that this image is consistent in brand, and looks professional.

Company cover photo: minimum 1,536 pixels wide x 768 pixels high; PNG/JPEG/GIF format; maximum size of file is 2MB.

...cont'd

Company cover photo

Avatar/company logo

Company logo: 400 x 400 pixels; PNG/JPEG/GIF format; maximum size of file is 2MB.

How do I add a logo and company cover photo?

To add or change your company cover image:

Click on the **Edit (pencil) icon** within the cover photo, then click **Upload cover image**. Choose the image you want to use from your files, then click Open.

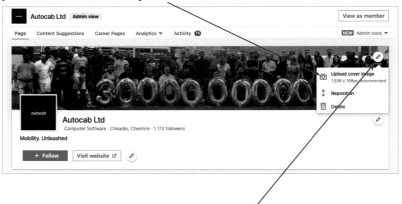

To add or change your company logo:

Click on the **Edit (pencil) icon** then select the logo image you want to use from your files, then click **Open**.

② Have you completed your company overview?

- The company name and description is picked up by search engines. Therefore, a full and complete company overview is essential.
- LinkedIn allows a maximum of 2,000 characters to be added to your company page overview, which is ample content.

To edit your company page overview

Edit	✕
Header	Provide details to display on your page
Page info	* indicates required
Buttons	Description*
About	Autocab – the No. 1 supplier of taxi booking & dispatch systems in the world
Overview	Having sold their first system in 1991, Autocab has grown to become the largest supplier of taxi systems in the world today. Their bespoke cloud-based SaaS
Locations	1483/2000

Click **Edit**, then add or edit your company description.

Within your company overview try to convey everything you can about the strength of your business, the staff who work for the organization, and any unique selling points you have.

This is your opportunity to allay any fears someone who has never heard about your business might have. What's your pedigree within the industry you operate? How and why are you qualified to fix the business challenges facing your customers?

If you're a startup, then celebrate the fact! Don't be shy to say how you are disrupting the market. Maybe you have a novel approach to working with clients. Whatever it is, this is the place to blow your own trumpet!

Hot tip

Ensure that your company description is complete, and make the most of your 2,000-character allowance with keyword rich content.

Always add a little "Update to" in the main update box to explain why you are sharing this particular link, or to give a call to action.

3 Have you customized content to the followers of your page?

Content that is customized to the followers of your page and your customers' professional interests certainly works best.

When posting an update, use concise introductions and eye-catching headlines. Make your content short. It needs to be appealing so that others will share the content with their connections. One of the easiest ways to encourage engagement is by adding an image, video or a link. If you do not have any of these to share, then consider asking questions that are relevant to your industry – for example, "How often do you post on LinkedIn?". There are various techniques to learn when posting an activity update on LinkedIn.

How do you add a status update?

Click on **Start a post** in the Update status area and type a standard text update.

But a text-only post will no doubt get lost in the noise. Therefore, it's important to do one (or more) of the following on each and every company post:

- Share a link to a website or sales page within the text post – LinkedIn will find the page and display an image from that page along with the headline.
- Add an image by clicking on the small camera icon.
- Add a video by clicking on the small video icon.
- Add a document by clicking on the small document icon.

There are some recommended techniques when adding a link to a status update within your company page, illustrated below:

- Copy and paste the URL (website address) from your original source. Once the details have been imported, you can delete the website address from the update. This gives the update a cleaner look.

- This whole area is editable. If you want to amend the title or any other text, simply click on the fields for the title and the description becomes editable.

Paste URL then delete once imported

Editable area

- You can choose to use the default image that LinkedIn has pulled through from the web address, or click on the camera icon and choose your own image.

Keep in mind that LinkedIn users will be checking your updates on multiple devices, so ensure that you are mixing your content on a regular basis.

Do all employees have their accounts linked to your page?

If you have a number of people in your team, then suggest they link their profiles to your company page. LinkedIn company pages were only introduced a few years ago. Therefore, if your employees were early users of LinkedIn then they may not have your company page linked to their personal profile.

If you are the owner of the business, then you may want to first take a look to see how many employees have linked their profile to your company page.

Checklist

How professional is your LinkedIn profile?

1 Have you included keywords within your professional headline? ☐

2 Have you labeled your websites correctly or do they still say "Company website"? ☐

3 Have you grabbed your unique URL? ☐

4 Have you added your Twitter account(s)? ☐

5 Do you have a completed summary and is it written in the first person with a full list of specialisms? ☐

6 Have you included rich text media in your profile summary? That is, have you added visuals, PDFs, slideshare presentations, videos, etc. to enhance your profile? ☐

7 Is your personal profile linked to your company page? ☐

8 Do you have a minimum of 10 skills listed? ☐

9 Do you have a minimum of 10 recommendations? ☐

10 Have you added "additional information" that is viewable to the public? ☐

14 Pinterest

A picture says a thousand words and Pinterest has quickly become the go-to destination for powerful imagery and the curation of ideas and themes. Help your customers make sense of the world and keep your brand front-of-mind.

What is Pinterest?

Pinterest is a tool for collecting and organizing the things that inspire you.

Millions of people are using Pinterest in their work and their daily lives. No matter what you are interested in, you will find an image of it on Pinterest.

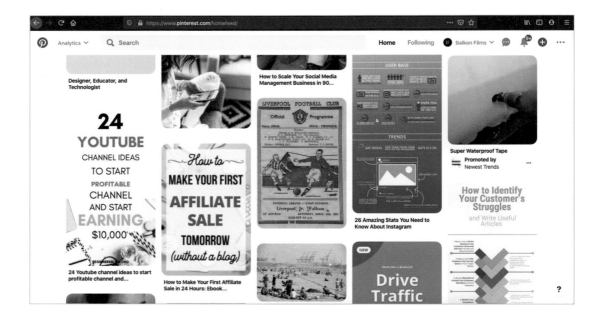

It is also a very vibrant social networking site, but to be strictly accurate, it is actually a social bookmarking site.

Hot tip

Pinterest was launched in 2010 and the clue to its philosophy lies in its name. Pinterest is a virtual pin board.

Is Pinterest important?

Pinterest is among the top 20 largest social networking sites. If your business is visual in any way, or you have an e-commerce site that sells products, a design portfolio, or if you produce regular content on your website (blogging or articles) then Pinterest will be a valuable platform for your business. Here are the five main reasons why you should consider Pinterest as part of your social media strategy:

Pinterest converts pinners into customers
The route to your website from Pinterest is just one click away (once you have pinned your image correctly).

This quote taken from the HubSpot website sums it up.

> *It has over 300 million monthly global users and boasts over 200 billion Pins. And it gets better. Research by ecommerce platform Shopify found that it was "the #2 source of all referral traffic to their site, that 93 percent of users were using it to plan their purchases, and that the average resulting order value was $50 (higher than any other social media source).*

Source: https://www.shopify.ca/blog/pinterest-marketing (April 2019)

Impressive stats for a corkboard!

Put simply, it is a huge marketing opportunity for e-commerce stores.

Pinterest drives traffic to your website
According to a survey by Shareaholic (**https://www.shareaholic.com/blog/search-engine-social-media-traffic-trends-report-2017/**), Pinterest continues to increase as a source of social traffic to sites, increasing 27.5% year on year. This is one reason why we recommend pinning your blogs and articles from your website. Every Pin can include a link back to a website. Therefore, the possibilities are endless.

Hot tip

Pinning your blog articles to Pinterest can result in fantastic referral traffic to your website.

Setting up a business account

There is currently very little difference between a personal account and a business account on Pinterest in terms of what you can do with boards and Pins. However, if you want to start advertising on Pinterest or you want to make use of their analytics tools, then you will need to create a business account.

There are two sets of terms associated with Pinterest. You can find the business terms here: **https://business.pinterest.com/en/business-terms-of-service** The personal terms are here: **https://policy.pinterest.com/en/terms-of-service**

If you already have a personal Pinterest account that you would like to migrate into a business account, then follow these steps:

 Visit **business.pinterest.com**, then click **Sign up** and complete the form.

 Or, if you already have a personal account, click on the ellipsis/three dots to reveal the drop-down menu and select **Add a free business account**.

Profile checklist

 1 **Does your Pinterest name include a keyword about your business, as well as your business name?**

Maryann Rizzo

I'm an interior designer and I'm told I have a great eye. I hope these images will INSPIRE YOU to design, cook, garden, entertain, dress, and travel IN STYLE! ~ email: CuratedStyle@gmail.com

✓ curatedstyle.tumblr.com/ ♀ Northeast USA

- Ensure your profile is completed in full.
- You have 160 characters in the **About your profile** section, so use this space wisely. Make sure that you keep it engaging and not overly keyword-y.
- Unlike LinkedIn and Facebook, your username on Pinterest can be changed as often as you wish. Your username forms the website address that will direct people to your Pinterest account.
- The location is also important. If you are a local business, then add the city or town as well as the country.

 2 **Claiming your website and other social media accounts**

...cont'd

Pinterest makes it easy to link your Pinterest account with your website and with Instagram, Etsy, and YouTube.

By "claiming" your website, you are officially linking your website to your Pinterest account. By doing so, you will receive attribution analytics that will provide more insight into which Pins and boards are driving traffic to your website, which in turn will help you create more of the content that works, and less of the content that doesn't. As a security measure, to "claim" your website you need to prove you own/manage the domain, and there are two ways to do this:

● Add an HTML tag by pasting a tag Pinterest provide into the <head> section of your index.html (home) page.
● Download an HTML file that you then need to upload to your website's root directory.

If you're not sure how to complete either of these methods, your developer will be able to do it for you.

You can also claim your Instagram, Etsy and YouTube accounts by clicking **Claim** – by doing this your profile name and picture will be added to your Pins from those accounts, which helps make your social footprint more "joined up" – both literally and figuratively.

3 Using notifications to grow your business

As busy business owners we try to do everything in our power to reduce clutter in our inboxes, but it's often a balance between reducing the amount of incoming notifications and staying abreast of what's happening in the industry and our business's social media accounts. So Pinterest notifications can be both a blessing and a curse, but if you're new to the platform and still figuring out how it can add value to your business, I'd advise turning on some or all notifications initially, and then turn off what's not working for you over the coming weeks.

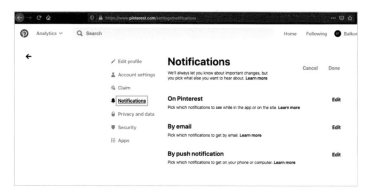

Pinterest offers a number of ways to receive notifications:

- **On Pinterest** – Alerts within the app or on your desktop. If you're regularly logging in to your Pinterest account, these notifications might be enough for you to see who's following you, and what activity is taking place.
- **Email notifications** – A digest of Pinterest activity emailed to you. Particularly useful if you follow your competitors, as you'll receive an email summary of who they're following and any new boards they create, which can provide a wealth of useful information about new products, strategies or pricing they might be employing.
- **Push notifications** – Alerts that appear on your mobile or desktop that highlight any activity on your account. By far the most aggressive of the notification options, push notifications can quickly prove to be unwieldy. However, if you're just getting started, then turn on push notifications for **Comments**, **Reactions**, and **Followers** so you can react quickly to any activity. Over time, depending on the volume of notifications, you can always elect to receive more or less.

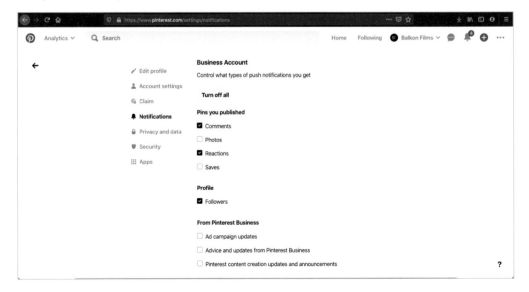

Adding a Pin to a board

To add a Pin to a board:

1 Click on the **Create pin** button

2 Drag and drop, or click to upload your image or video.

3 Find the board that you wish to change, click **Edit**, then change or add the description by completing the field as shown below:

4 Once the picture or video is uploaded, select which board you would like to allocate the image to, add a description and choose if you would like to publish immediately or at a later date.

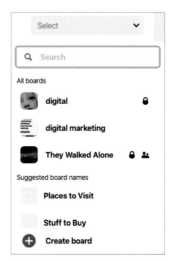

If you would like to add a website link to an image that you have uploaded from your computer, then you will need to complete the **Add a destination link** field.

Once you click **Publish**, your image will appear in the newsfeed to be showcased to your network. To find the image again, simply click on your board.

This is also the area where you can delete the Pin if you no longer wish to have it showcased on your Pinterest account. Click on the pencil icon and then click **Delete**.

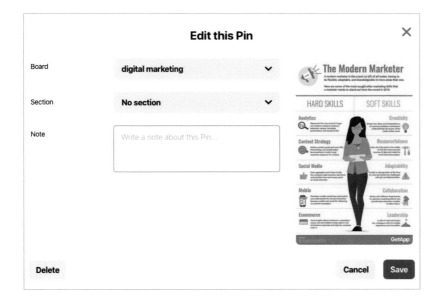

Sharing Pins

To share a Pin or board on another social network, follow the instructions below:

Sharing a Pin to a social network:

 Find the Pin on your board and click **Send** in the top left-hand corner of the Pin.

 Select the social network you want to share the Pin to.

 Follow the steps to log in, then write a description and share your Pin.

Sharing a board to a social network:

 From your profile, open the board you want to share.

 Click over the board title.

 Select the social network you want to share the board to.

 Follow the steps to log in, then write a description and share your board.

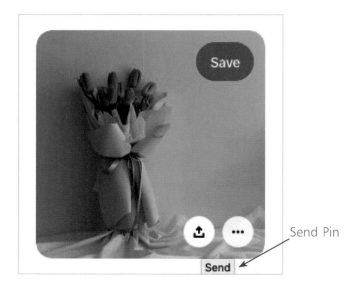

Send Pin

Browser integration

The easiest way to build up your Pins is to download a browser button. Visit **https://about.pinterest.com/en/browser-button** and you will be offered a button for whichever browser you are using (in the case below, Firefox).

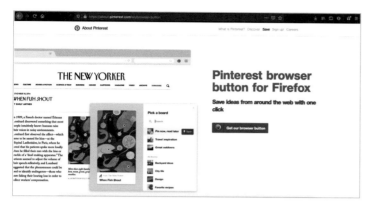

Browser buttons makes it easy to pin anything to your pin boards from any website whilst you're browsing the internet, rather than you having to keep returning to Pinterest every time you find something cool online.

Browser button

It is highly addictive

Pinterest is one of those social networking platforms that is highly addictive, and once you start pinning, you can't stop. This results in a highly engaged audience and is very powerful for business.

As Pinterest is a visual platform, it is easy to absorb information quickly, which is possibly the main reason it has become so successful.

Individual Pin checklist

Pinterest is introducing new Pin variations all the time, so it is worth subscribing to the Pinterest blog to make sure that you are keeping up with new opportunities. Visit **https://business.pinterest. com/en-gb/blog**

Here are the basic checks for your individual Pins:

 Does each Pin have a description?

It is imperative to check that your Pins have a description as this is picked up on the Pinterest search and also by other search engines.

 Check the source of your Pin

Pinterest is in the public domain and, therefore, copyright rules still apply. Check the small print for Pinterest copyright by visiting **http://about.pinterest.com/copyright/**

Checking the source of your Pin is extremely important. Always check the source of your Pin if you are re-pinning others' content. If you click on the Pin and the landing page is a false URL, or an error site, then do not re-pin it. You can also report it or leave a comment on the Pin to warn others. Sometimes, pinners will use a popular image, but then the source of the Pin will lead to their own website rather than the site of the original source. This is unethical pinning and, therefore, do not re-pin and only give credit where credit is due.

 Have you added a watermark?

If you are creating your own images, then consider adding a stamp or watermark. This way, the content will always stay connected to your brand and will continue to promote you whenever the post is re-pinned. It is also a deterrent for others who wish to use your image, but not give you the credit for it.

If you are not a designer, but you still wish to add a watermark to your Pins, then have a look at a free and easy-to-use tool called PicMonkey: **http://www.picmonkey.com/**

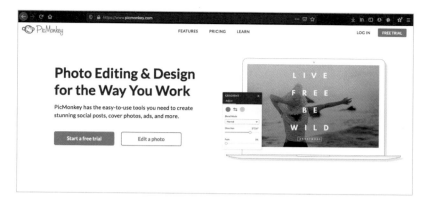

 4 **Take advantage of Rich Pins**

Pinterest offers Rich Pins for products, articles, recipes and movies to any brand. If you add a Rich Pin, then you have the opportunity to pin much more information on the Pin than regular Pins. It is not a simple process to add Rich Pins to your account.

To find out how, visit **https://developers.pinterest.com/rich_pins/**

 5 **Are your Pins optimized for Twitter?**

You may not be tweeting your Pins, but others may! Try to keep your descriptions under 280 characters and utilize hashtags within your descriptions. Make it easy for others to share your content with their audience.

Mastering Pinterest boards

To create a board

Pinterest boards are where you collect Pins. For example, if you were refurbishing your office, then you may have a Pinterest board called "Office refurb ideas". When you see an image (or Pin) of a desk or a cupboard that would look great in your new office, then you would pin the image to your board. You then build your boards with your collection of images.

1 Select **Boards** and then click on the **Create board** button.

Make sure that each board has a full description, including some good keywords. Choose a category and then add a location if needed.

You will see the option for a secret board. A secret board can be shared with other selected pinners and is not in the public domain. A secret board can be used for a number of reasons, such as organizing a surprise party, showcasing ideas for a new project that has not yet been launched, or even as a Christmas gift list. You can have unlimited secret boards.

You can add new boards from your profile or while you're pinning, and you can always edit a board if you ever need to change its name or description.

Does each board have a description?

If you have existing boards, then please go back and see if they have a full description. If you created your Pinterest boards a while ago, then it is worth checking all of your boards to make sure that they have a description.

Originally, Pinterest would not allow descriptions at the initial stage of creation. Therefore, there are many boards out there that do not have a full description. The description of your board is a key aspect to being found in the search results.

To add or change a description to a board that has already been created, follow these instructions:

To maximize search results, make sure that you have added a description to your Pinterest boards.

 Click on **Boards** to see all of your boards.

 Find the board that you wish to change, and click on the **Edit** (pencil) icon.

...cont'd

3 Change or add the description by completing the fields as shown below.

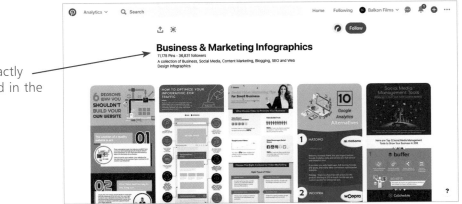

Do you have relatively short titles?

Boards with shorter titles are more likely to be followed. Active pinners are usually very visual people, and not necessarily big readers. Therefore, having short and to-the-point titles for your boards will give you an advantage over other pinners.

Title explains exactly what's contained in the board

Do you have a minimum of five Pins in each of your boards?

It is best not to launch a board unless you have a minimum of five Pins. Not only does the board look a little unloved if it has only one lonely Pin sitting there, but it also gives the impression that you are not an active pinner.

Do you have a minimum of five boards?

If you do not have a minimum of five boards, then your Pinterest account will appear inactive and very new. So, this is your first goal. Choose topics or categories that reflect your business values, culture, interests, products, and services. Be creative with your board names!

If you are a business owner, then here are a few ideas of popular boards to get you started. Remember to pin as much from your website as possible.

- The blog
- Books worth reading
- Quotations
- Infographics
- Meet the team
- Guest bloggers
- Facebook pictures
- Our products
- Our services
- Portfolios
- Technology
- Things I like

Implementing a content strategy

Pinterest is no different from any other marketing and you need to plan your content, engagement and listening strategy to be an effective marketer on this platform. Here are some strategies to consider:

Research
Have a look at others within your industry to see what they are pinning, but also have a look at your target market to see what type of images are of interest to them and which boards they have set up. Look at your emails. Are you often answering questions to solve people's problems? If so, then consider adding a board where you can showcase these answers.

Searching on Pinterest is easy.

 Enter your search term.

 Select from Pins, Boards or Pinners.

Hot tip

You need to let people know that you exist, and following others is a good way to start. You will be amazed how many people will follow you back as soon as you start repinning their content. It is also a good source of content for your own boards.

Remember your boards
It can be too easy to forget some boards that you have created, as you will find yourself pinning to certain boards on a more regular basis. Make a conscious effort to pin across a range of boards as this will stretch your imagination and keep your boards alive.

Remember to follow other pinners
Search and follow other users or individual boards that are of interest to you.

From the Search box at the top of your Pinterest account, you can find results for P0ins (default), Boards or Pinners. This is the main reason why you should be adding descriptions to your Pins, boards and profiles.

Remember to add website addresses to your descriptions

The more information about the source of a Pin, the better it is for website traffic and general brand awareness.

Check ALL your Pins

Whether you are re-pinning or you are creating your own Pins, always double check the Pin to make sure that the link works.

Do not Pin-overload!

It is tempting to spend time on Pinterest and then pin many images in one go, but refrain from doing this as you will flood your newsfeed and your audience will not be happy.

Time your Pins

When are your followers online the most? The easiest way to find out is to take a look at a company called Tailwind:
http://www.tailwindapp.com/

As part of your Pinterest strategy, consider using some Pinterest scheduling tools such as the Viraltag application within Hootsuite, or Viralwoot (**https://viralwoot.com/**).

If you can post your blog or new products at the times that your network is online the most, then how powerful will that be for your business?

Produce pinnable content

80% of all Pins are re-pins, so make sure that your own content has the "re-pin factor".

Add fabulous images to your blog

If you start investing in images for each blog article, you are likely to see a dramatic increase in the traffic from Pinterest to your website.

Need some stock images for your Pins? No problem. Check out **www.pexels.com** for a selection of royalty-free images.

Have a play with different sizes

Tall Pins are more noticeable in the newsfeed, but try not to make them too long. The recommended Pin dimensions are 600 pixels x 900 pixels. If you are using a different width, just make sure that it is a 2:3 ratio.

Conclusion

1 Build your platform

Have you created a business Pinterest account that has been edited correctly? Do you have at least five boards that all have a minimum of five Pins within them? Have you chosen a cover photo for each of those boards? Have you verified your website and received the check mark on your account? Have you pinned the key features of your business to your Pinterest account from your website? Have you added the Pin it button to your website and social sharing tools? If you can say "yes" to the majority of the above, then congratulations – you have reached stage one of Pinterest success.

2 Grow your network

Have you emailed your database to let them know about your Pinterest account? Have you added a link to your email signature? Have you added a Pinterest icon with a link on your website? Have you followed people within your target market? Have you also commented and re-pinned others' content to engage with your audience? Do you have a strategy to cross-promote your Pins on Facebook, Twitter and other social networking platforms? Do you embed your Pinterest boards into your blog articles? Utilizing collaborative boards will help with growing your network on Pinterest.

Pinterest can be a slow burn to get your number of followers increased significantly. Therefore, do not expect thousands of followers immediately. It takes time to build, but the investment is worth it.

If you are investing time in the above strategies to grow your network, then congratulations – you have reached stage two of Pinterest success.

3 Implement a strategy

Once you have your initial boards created, then it is time to consider your strategy for pinning and engagement.

Have you done your research? Do you have a strategy to check those forgotten boards? Do you have a strategy to follow other pinners? Do you check all Pins for correct links? Are you pinning consistently? Do you know the best time of the day to pin those important sales Pins? Are you utilizing design tools to give your Pins the "re-pin factor"? Are you adding fabulous images to your blog? Have you experimented with different-sized images to see what works best on your account? Are you promoting your Pins through contents? Have you joined any community boards?

If you have a defined written strategy that is being implemented for Pinterest, then congratulations – you have now reached stage three of Pinterest success.

Measure the results

Pinterest offers users a powerful analytics tool. This is completely free of charge and will enlighten you with many analytics, such as metrics about the people who engage with your business and other topics that they are interested in. You can also view your audience's most common interests at a glance and you can tailor your marketing strategy around this information.

If you are a numbers person, then you will probably enjoy the statistics on number of impressions, re-pins and clicks.

The analytics tool is only available to those that have registered a business account. Simply go to **https://analytics.pinterest.com/** to find out your statistics.

If you are measuring your results, tweaking your strategy to improve those results, then congratulations – you have reached stage four of Pinterest success.

Remember, it is OK if your Pinterest account does not have a million followers, because it takes time to build something amazing. Just keep engaging with your users, putting out great content and being a good member of the Pinterest community, and your hard work will be rewarded.

Checklist

Have a look at the checklist below and see how you have scored.

 Have you set up a business account?

 Have you verified (claimed) your website?

 Does your Pinterest name include a keyword about your business, as well as your business name?

 Do you have a minimum of five Pinterest boards?

 Does each board have a full description?

 Do you have relatively short titles for your boards?

 Do you have a minimum of five Pins in each of your boards?

 Does each individual Pin have a full description?

 Do your Pins contain a content source? (i.e. Does it link to a website?)

 Are you posting a mix of images and videos?

15 Google Analytics

The beauty of digital is everything is trackable, traceable and accountable. Google's powerful business intelligence platform offers users unprecedented access to data about your website and visitors.

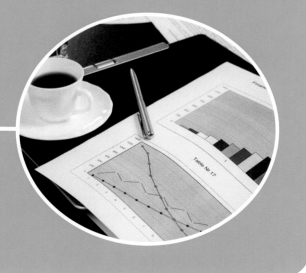

An introduction to Analytics

You may have designed an excellent website, put into play some great content marketing and marketing automation, and developed a strong presence across your various social channels. Yet, if you've got no real idea about who is visiting your website, where they're coming from, what drove them to click through to your site, which pages they're visiting, how long they are staying on your website (and why and when they're leaving your site), you may be wasting tons of cash and energy on targeting the wrong kind of audience.

You need to grasp the answers to those necessary queries in order to optimize your website and build it in an effective manner.

This is precisely where Google Analytics (GA) will be of great comfort, because it will ultimately help you in observing your website traffic. Hence, you'll be able to gain knowledge, improve your site's performance, and guarantee your conversion rates keep increasing.

Google Analytics is a web analytics and business intelligence tool, provided free of charge by Google.

Why do I need Google Analytics?

For all your online business data (blogs, articles, site content, and website designs and layouts), you do market research to discover what people are fond of and what they search or prefer to look for. Thus, you try to construct your site keeping in mind your target audience. But, what if after doing everything right, you still don't get "that traffic" you wanted?

It is, no doubt, very important to plan and construct. But once your web pages are live, and your content marketing is being utilized and you're paying for ads, it is super important to keep a close eye on what is happening and why. Google Analytics gives you that helicopter view of your digital marketing – it analyzes your website for free, and brings you insights across your entire digital footprint.

When you have a full understanding of what your website is doing, when it's doing it and why, then you will know what you need to do to drive growth.

Let's take a look at how to create or set up Google Analytics.

Beware

To get the most out of Google Analytics consider paying a freelancer or agency to set up and manage your Analytics account, at least initially.

Setting up your account

You need to log in or create an account on Google (a Gmail account) to set up the account on the Google Analytics platform.

Note: You can only log in to the Google Analytics platform through a Google account ID. You can either create a new account on Google or you can use an existing Google account. Many prefer to use their Gmail accounts or IDs they use for Google Drive or the Google Play store.

Create a Google Analytics account

1 Open the Google Analytics platform (**https://analytics. google.com/**) and click on the **Create account** button.

The options on the left-hand sidebar are explained on page 280.

Beware

If you are running a multilingual website, consider a separate account ID for each language version, to keep the data separate.

...cont'd

The options on the left-hand sidebar of the Google Analytics homepage are as follows:

Home – Main panel of Google Analytics; displays a top-level overview of your website performance.

Customization – Tailor how the data is presented to you. Bring the statistics and key performance indicators (KPIs) that matter to you most to the forefront, and create your own customized reports and dashboards.

Realtime – See who is visiting your website right now: which pages they're on; where they're from; how they found your website; and which content is working.

Audience – Who is visiting your website over time: demographics; location; the device/s they're using; their behavior on your website; and their lifetime value to your business.

Acquisition – Learn how visitors are finding you. In terms of organic (free) traffic, which sites are referring you or what are users searching for and in terms of SEM (paid traffic), and which channels and advertising campaigns are working best.

Behavior – Deep dive into what visitors are doing on your website: which pages are the most popular; how long visitors spend on your web pages; and which pages are sending visitors away.

Conversions – Manage your web pages like your sales staff: find out what's converting users into consumers and which pages are making money.

Attribution – If you advertise with Google, turn on Attribution to better distribute credit to all ad clicks that led to a conversion.

Discover – Find apps, training, and certified partners to help you master Google Analytics. Both free and paid-for services are provided by Google and third parties.

Admin – The administration panel. All of your Google Analytics settings in one place.

2 Enter the name of your account – usually your business name.

3 Select the type you want to track – website or apps or apps and web.

4 Insert your website's URL (the property you wish to analyze).

5 Select your industry type.

6 Set the time zone.

7 Click **Create**. You will then be asked to agree to the "Google Analytics Terms of Service Agreement", and "Additional Terms Applicable to Data Shared with Google".

8 Once you click **I accept,** you'll be presented with your website's unique tracking code.

Tracking code

If you have reached this step, it means you have set up your account successfully. Now, get your tracking code from Google Analytics that you need to apply on each page of your website that you wish to track:

1 Select **Admin** from the left-hand panel.

2 Select **Tracking Info** under the Property column.

3 Click on the **Tracking Code** option – a window like the one shown below will open, which shows the tracking code. You need to copy the whole code and paste it to your websites' pages to be tracked.

282

Note – in this step, you can proceed with the tracking code setup in three ways:

- Do it yourself (if you have access to your web server and know how to add code to a web page) or speak to your web designer who will add the tracking code (script) to the relevant areas of your website and set you up with an account and reports.

- Create tags and triggers through your Google Tag Manager account.

- If you have a WordPress-based website, install and activate the plugin to get the job done automatically.

Measuring success

When you first log in to Google Analytics, it can be rather daunting. Here are the top six aspects that all business owners should measure:

Visitors

Figuring out how your website is being used, and using information to enhance your site, ultimately starts with the visitor. Knowing who is coming to visit your site, how long they then spend on the site, and which pages they are looking at before leaving can give you valuable insight into improving the functionality of your site.

Four metrics to look at on this overview report on a regular basis are:

- Sessions.
- Average session duration.
- Bounce rate.
- New visitors.

It will take a few weeks of running your Analytics account to really begin to reap the rewards.

Sessions

This signifies the visitors that have spent any time on your website. The reason you should pay more attention to this statistic, rather than page views, is because you want to know that people are exploring your site, and that they are not "bots" or spam accounts.

Average session duration

You need to know that people are exploring your site and spending some quality time reading content. If your average session is under 30 seconds, then you know you need to add more relevant and engaging content to your site.

...cont'd

Bounce rate

Bounce rate is the measurement of people who stay on your website for a short amount of time. It is rumored that the level set for Google Analytics' bounce rate is 30 seconds. However, Google has never announced this. If you have a high bounce rate of 80%, it means that people have visited your website for 30 seconds or less and then navigated to another website.

Many people ask "What should my bounce rate be?". There isn't a right answer to that question, as every industry and audience is different. Sometimes a high bounce rate is not a bad thing. For example, if you want people to instantly sign up for your newsletter or download an ebook on that first initial page visit, then your bounce rate will be high, but you have converted a number of visitors.

New visitors

It is important to ensure that your audience is growing consistently and that new people are visiting your website. Having a fine balance between returning visitors and brand new visitors is important. Ultimately, you should watch your visitor metrics for major dips and peaks.

Acquisition

This is Google's language for "traffic sources". It is important to know where your traffic is coming from. Click **Acquisition** in the left-hand column on Google Analytics' Overview page.

Having a healthy balance of search, referral and direct traffic is good for your business.

If you have over 80% organic search or paid search traffic, and Google makes an algorithm change, you can lose money extremely quickly.

If you explore further into your All Traffic > Source/Medium report, you can see which sources sent the most traffic. The Social report is always intriguing, but you may also be interested to explore the other areas.

If you look at the individual source reports, you can see All Traffic, Direct, Referrals, Search and Campaigns. Campaigns is where your pay-per-click accounts should live.

Bounce rates

Index